CN2 LT

320.0941
NA1

PARIAH

PARIAH

Misfortunes of the
British Kingdom

◆

TOM NAIRN

VERSO

London • New York

First published by Verso 2002
© Tom Nairn
All rights reserved

1 3 5 7 9 10 8 6 4 2

Verso
UK: 6 Meard Street, London W1F 0EG
US: 180 Varick Street, New York, NY 10014–4606
www.versobooks.com

Verso is the imprint of New Left Books

ISBN 1–85984–657–2

British Library Cataloguing in Publication Data
A catalogue record for this book is available from the British Library

Library of Congress Cataloging-in-Publication Data
A catalog record for this book is available from the Library of Congress

Typeset in Minion by M Rules
Printed by Biddles Ltd, Guildford and King's Lynn
www.biddles.co.uk

A pariah King . . .
Who cut himself off from his own kind
Even though Almighty God had made him
Eminent and powerful and marked him from the start
For a happy life . . .
His old possessions seem paltry to him now.
He covets and resents, dishonours custom
And bestows no gold, and because of good things
That the Heavenly Powers gave him in the past
He ignores the shape of things to come.

Beowulf, lines 1715–50
Translated by Seamus Heaney, 2001

What we are witnessing has all the dignity of a punter waiting around
outside a betting shop, eventually summoning the courage to go in . . .
Anthony Barnett, *Newsletter* of Charter 88
(speaking of the 1987 UK election)

For Paul, Stephanie, Joel and Alan,
who made the Austral Shore a home

CONTENTS

Foreword   IX

1   Election as Pantomime   1
2   Changeling Kingdom   14
3   Mythological Greatness   32
4   The Glow from the Past   50
5   The Threat of Ordinariness   60
6   Hair-shirt Britishness   71
7   Constitutional Arthritis   80
8   The Watchdogs   88
9   The Incomer's Dilemma   98
10 Last-gasp Britons   111
11 Folies de Grandeur   124
12 Dr Britain and Mr England, or: More Dirty Pool?   138

    Epilogue 2002   147
    Appendix   163
    Index   171

FOREWORD

This book was begun during the interminable New Labour campaign for the British General Election of June 2001; but most of it was finished around the time of the Australian General Election of 10 November 2001. These two cumulative experiences made me feel something was fishy, in the state of more than Hamlet's Denmark. Both tragi-comedies followed closely upon the surreal farce of George W. Bush's non-election as President of the USA. Yet by the time *Pariah* went to press, 'the West' had embarked on a worldwide War against Terrorism. Crypto-President Bush has by his side the triumphal Tony Blair (re-elected by an overwhelming quarter of the UK electorate) and the equally refulgent John Howard (whose re-election hinged upon squalid lies about asylum-seeking refugees drowning their children). A question posed itself: somewhere, is there not a bigger fish rotting from the head downwards? Has 'globalisation' (inexorable if chastening March of Progress, etc.) somehow rebounded upon its own forgers in the West? This doubt formed the context in which the absurdities of Tony Blair's 2001 re-election came to be viewed in the following essay.

Writing it would have been impossible without the support of the Joseph Rowntree Reform Trust, of York, England, from 2000 to July 2001. I am very grateful for their help, and especially for the personal encouragement and suggestions of Trevor Smith. Pam Giddy of Charter 88 in

London, Anthony Barnett and David Hayes of OpenDemocracy.net, Gerry Hassan in Scotland and John Osmond in Wales supplied non-stop inspiration. The later stages of the book were written partly at Monash University in Melbourne, for which I must thank Peter Spearritt and his School of Political and Social Inquiry, as well as Paul James and the others mentioned in my dedication. Latterly much encouragement has come from my new colleagues in and around the Globalism Research Centre at RMIT University: Mary Kalantzis, Michael Singh, Christopher Ziguras and Peter Phipps. Moral support also came from Tom Devine's Research Institute in Irish and Scottish Studies at the University of Aberdeen, Scotland. Great practical backing has come at all stages from Jonathan Williams and his Literary Agency in Dun Laoghaire, Dublin. At Verso Books and the *New Left Review* I owe a great deal to Susan Watkins, Perry Anderson and Tariq Ali, notably for their patience over the months of July and August 2001, when I was combining re-writing with moving to Melbourne. Millicent Petrie helped me with the latter, and neither the move nor the book would have got far without her. Many different families have been involved in the genesis of what follows; but Millicent, Rachel and Greig are the most important ones.

Department of Language and International Studies,
Royal Melbourne Institute of Technology,
Swanston Street
Melbourne, Victoria, Australia.

1 ELECTION AS PANTOMINE

'Pariah': native mongrel of North Africa or South Asia, varying greatly
in conformation and important chiefly as a scavenger.
'Pariahdom': the condition of being a pariah: 'They walked on together
and I dropped behind, suddenly realizing my pariahdom' – W.J. Locke
Webster's Dictionary 1986

The United Kingdom was promised a General Election from the very
beginning of the year 2001. Repeating the pattern predicted in 1990 by
Anthony Barnett (he was dreading what turned out to be the election of
1992) the punters began to gather around the bookmaker's door from
February 2001 onwards. So determined was Blair's New Labour government to stage the event that months were spent softening up the voters
with leaden hints and 'speculations'. Within five-year limits, the timing of
British electoral debauches is decided by the government in power, rather
than by a written constitution or a President. We see at once that the
putrefaction of the British State is by no means confined to back rooms
and pockets. The stigmata of Pariahdom are borne proudly on its fore-
head, and manifested even through secondary 'conventions' like this one.
So the voters had to be over-informed that the moment chosen – early
May – was positively overdue, and not merely 'timely'. It became practically
inevitable, like writing on the wall of fate. Nothing must stand in Mr
Blair's way.

Until something did, that is: the virtual shut-down of the British countryside by an epidemic of foot-and-mouth disease, from March onwards.

Subsequent comparisons showed this to be the worst recorded outbreak of the disease anywhere.[1] But it was at first impatiently disregarded by the government, as if Omar Khayyam's Moving Finger had wobbled slightly, and should be corrected. At last things got so bad, with so many indications of voter resentment and apathy, that Prime Minister Blair found the message had to be reinscribed. The moment of triumph proved after all postponable. A short delay until June was agreed, with extreme reluctance, and against great opposition from within his party. And finally the punters were allowed to rush into the shop for a 'campaign' leading up to the 7th of June.

Why this mixture of haste and stubbornness? The likely explanation is because the New Labour government was conscious of the ground shifting away from beneath it – not so much towards the official Conservative Opposition, as simply towards 'apathy', a somewhat terminal-looking evaporation of the remarkable enthusiasm that had greeted New Labour immediately after its 1997 victory. And yet, this sense of foreboding and indifference to Blair's interminably vaunted British Renaissance is anything but self-explanatory.

Events alone never appeared to justify it. There was indeed some apprehension about the gathering United States recession, but in early 2001 no economic disaster seemed imminent. Although the broader economic situation did get worse over the election months, opinion surveys over the same time showed most United Kingdomers quite sanguine about their prospects *as individuals* – at least in the South-East and other prosperous

---

1   It signalled in fact what Andrew O'Hagan has called in a subsequent book *The End of British Farming* (Profile Books 2001). O'Hagan is concerned rightly with the end of one aspect of British identity – 'the heady, long-standing, romantic and sworn place in the British cultural imagination' which came to an end simultaneously with the General Election of 7 June 2001.

patches. And yet, they were simultaneously becoming stubbornly and increasingly cynical about 'politics' and the state.

When June arrived, fresh outbreaks of the great epidemic were still occurring, and in parts of Britain voters were obliged to disinfect themselves before entering the polling stations. More significantly (one might have thought), the slaughter of three million animals now had a history to it – one which revealed a bewildering chronicle of governmental incompetence from Day One of the disaster. So postponement turned out to have its own inconveniences. The national will would now be called upon to pronounce, not only among mountain-ranges of decaying carcasses but amid angry calls for the abolition of the body responsible, the Ministry of Agriculture, Food & Fisheries. And yet, New Labour was still voted back. In the quaint terminology of Ukanian elections, it enjoyed a second 'landslide' victory.

This is a conjuncture of events so weird that special explanation is called for. As journalist Nick Cohen, one of England's most acute commentators, wrote well before the vote: 'The biggest story of the campaign . . . will be *what doesn't happen*'. He even thought that the 2001 election would go on to 'mark the death of representative government in Britain' (*Observer*, 25 March). 'Cynicism from above breeds cynicism from below', wrote Cohen, the author of *Cruel Britannia* (1999): 'This election will mark the moment when it will no longer be possible to pretend that Westminster represents the population'. After the vote, only Cohen's verb tense had to be changed. The results would show how misrepresentation has become chronic, but also somehow settled – if anything, less shakeable than before June 2001.

So, the assumptions and climate of 2001 mattered much more than what happened or failed to happen on polling day – a point that was to be underlined by the miserable voting figures on the 7th of June, as well as by the sour atmosphere of doom and confusion linked to the foot-and-mouth epidemic. Less calculable things must have been happening upon another level altogether, in spite of a government so devoted to zealous calculation and over-anxious control. A deeper, more massive current was running beneath the trite froth and platitudes of what the English still, in memory of centuries past, call 'the hustings'.[2] But what was this malaise – and what will become of it now, as New Labour moves into its second term?

Naturally, Blair's government sought vigorously to conceal it on the plane of display and official ostentation – the *société du spectacle* of which Blairism has been such a champion. Here, the terrain had been prepared as thoroughly as possible by Blair's first government, and not just in terms of campaign strategy. Since the end of 2000, all the pressures and appeal of his government had been directed towards the comfortably retrograde. Although Young Britain still figured occasionally in régime rhetoric, evocations of business-as-usual had by this time supplanted the earlier giddy elation of Coolness and the Dome. It was Chancellor Brown's funereal solidity that dominated the Westminster scene. The person and spirit of former Northern Ireland Secretary Peter Mandelson were replaced by those of the sombre Dr John Reid (and not in Belfast alone). The people were certainly thoroughly warmed up, prior to being (in the Brechtian sense) 're-elected'.

Anthony Barnett has compared British elections to a fling at the bookmaker's: staggering into a betting-shop to lose one's shirt. But they also resemble family visits to a very traditional music hall or vaudeville. On the 'hustings', ancestral echoes and nostalgia for times past are supposed to take over. All British modernisation is built upon nostalgia. Funeral pyres

---

2 *Shorter Oxford English Dictionary* (1986): 'The temporary platform on which candidates for Parliament formerly stood for nomination, and while addressing the electors. Hence, the proceedings at a parliamentary election. 1719'.

and pits notwithstanding, the British voters found themselves ushered back towards this old election-time Music Hall from early spring onwards. They took their 2001 seats for the traditional 'swingometer' pantomine, as it were, while the orchestra tuned up and the reassuring chink of glasses resounded from the interval bar. The management knows that once bums are on seats, people stay there. In a geographical simple-majority system, a kind of insane suspense is inseparable from the show. Hundreds of small first-past-the-post Punch and Judy shows unfold. Most are foregone conclusions, but many come with cheap thrills and surprising walk-on parts. Above all in the 'marginals', there is some uncertainty as to who will kill whom.

Although nobody thought New Labour would lose, Mr Blair had declared war against 'apathy' early on. He could not merely fail to lose. A Magus needs to win big, and Blair let it be known that his impatience had grown. In spite of – or possibly because of – indifferent success with some opening chapters, he now yearned to bear the Third Way narrative forward. Many in his court clearly feared (rightly enough) that in tune with New Labour's general infatuation for things American, British voting abstention might slump down to US levels. That would undermine Blair's spell, as well as being a betrayal of the Liberties our forefathers fought for.

London's commentating trusties certainly did their best to stir up the delicious uncertainty of yore. Tales of great past performances and pantomime Dames resounded once more. Since foregone conclusions make poor theatre, the public had to be reminded of turnarounds and pitfalls. Had not the British story since 1719 (or thereabouts) recorded many a startling upset, and plenty of *volte-faces*? Few of these were left in peace over April and May 2001. Two months before the vote I recall seeing on a single day two clips of Mrs Thatcher's 1979 victory speech on TV, plus one haunting each from Harold Wilson (1964), Edward Heath (1970) and – lest we forget – Michael Foot (1983). And that was in Scotland, whose television is these days sometimes spared the worst.

Once settled in their places, the public was treated to another session of stage mesmerism, something like the one so unforgettably described by Thomas Mann in *Mario and the Magician* (1929). Mann was evoking 1920s Italy, through an old-fashioned pier-show and its sinister star, the Cavaliere Cipolla – he could not then have imagined *Big Brother* or *The Weakest Link*:

> While [the magician] still practiced some rhetorical circumlocutions, the tests themselves were one long series of attacks upon the will-power, the loss or compulsion of volition. Comic, exciting, amazing by turns, by midnight they were still in full swing; we ran the gamut of all the phenomena this natural–unnatural field has to show, from the unimpressive at one end of the scale to the monstrous at the other . . .[3]

Mann noted that the Italian public knew, or half-knew, how the vile hypnotist was at once leading and humiliating them, and yet remained quite unable to do anything other than conform. Even at the mercy of the uncanny, they felt compelled to let 'nature' take its course. The weekly *Spectator*'s cartoonist 'Heath' had the same idea in its number of 21 May 2001, with a drawing of Blair as a stage hypnotist sending his audience to sleep with the message: 'I want you to stay asleep until election day. Then, when I snap my fingers, I want you to go out and vote New Labour . . .'.

In part the election's unreality may of course have derived from the

---

3   Thomas Mann, *Mario and the Magician and Other Stories* (Vintage Classics edition 2000), pp. 145–6.

prior collapse of so much of Britain's fabric. The acrid smoke still hanging around on polling day should not, and plainly did not, make the hypnotised voters forget all the shames of yesterday. The Passport Scandal, BSE, CJD, the grim farce of the asylum-seekers, the tale of the Dome, the continuing slide of the Health Service, the state of HM's Prison Service, Railtrack's collapse, the Fuel Crisis of September 2000, the Hinduja brothers scandal: Britannia Music Hall was in sensationally poor shape well before March 2001.

Just how poor was beginning to impress many foreign observers. The Music Hall audience was perturbed by a German verdict towards the end of May, when Bernd Dörler of *Stern* magazine unfolded 'The English Patient', a twelve-page denunciation of Blairland. Four years ago 'the shiny Tony stepped up with his successful wife and small children, thrilling the people with his talk of a Third Way and Cool Britannia'. Now instead, an 'apocalyptic state of affairs' prevailed, with thousands of tourists staying away from Heritage Britain, and much of it viewed as 'dangerous, unsafe territory':

> More than the billions of pounds lost is the self-confidence of the British, the realization they have the scorn and the mockery of 'bloody foreigners'. The United Kingdom, in the words of the Irish Economics Minister, is again 'the Leper of Europe'. The *New York Times* called Britain the Epidemic Island, while the Italian *L'Espresso* said a curse lay over this land . . .[4]

In this wave of bad-mouthing, even the *Wall Street Journal* lost faith. With a recent series it contributed its own note of prim disillusion to the British

---

4 Dörler's article was reproduced in the *Scotsman* of 24 May and the *Sunday Times* of 27 May 2001.

pre-electoral gloom, detecting almost nothing but 'decline and fall', the disjointed antics of an embarassing junior partner. This is a state that can't decide whether it's European or American, was the Editorial diagnosis – the result being a 'compromise' that enshrines the worst aspects of both.[5] Sure, George W. Bush's USA needs allies – but wouldn't another organ-grinder be better than a monkey like this?

Once upon a time people viewed the collapsing Ottoman imperium as 'the sick man of Europe'. But they rarely went as far as these recent denigrators. The Sultanate had been in decline for as long as anyone could remember, and little had come to be expected of it. Shiny Tony and Cool Britannia had in contrast promised a lot, loudly and recently. Fondness for Her Majesty's domain is not yet confined to the equivalent of 'Orientalists', although there had certainly been a drift in that direction. By 2001 even the most blinkered of Ukanian well-wishers had begun to re-think earlier judgements. They could now hardly help (for example) turning from Westminster's hustings and bewigged rituals to confront Oldham, beset by race riots during the election, with 16 per cent of the voters backing the racialist 'British National Party'; or a White-Cliffs Dover griping about 'asylum-seekers', and what the Institute of Race Relations has so well described as 'The Dispersal of Xenophobia'.[6]

In fact pre-electoral anathemas were by no means confined to outside commentators. They have been getting pretty routine at home. One of Britain's most revered political columnists, Alan Watkins, delivered himself thus:

---

5 As summarised in *The Week* (London), 21 March 2001.

6 Institute of Race Relations, 'Online Resources', *'The Dispersal of Xenophobia': a Special Report on the UK and Ireland*, by Liz Fekete, at http://www.homebeats.co.uk/dispersal/index.htm.

When Mr Tony Blair confided to the *Sun* newspaper before he told the cabinet (or for that matter the Queen) that he was postponing the election until June 7th, the feel-bad factor was undoubtedly high. The pyres were burning, the rainstorms dreadful; the railways collapsing; the hospitals filthy, with the doctors killing innocent civilians indiscriminately ... even the Liberal Democrats appear to have abandoned their promise to re-nationalize the railways, and at the end of the tunnel there is nothing but gloom. (*Independent*, 26 May 2001)

Mr Watkins's style of exaggeration was unimportant here. He was only echoing an intensifying popular mood. Nothing seemed able to dispel the foreboding and indifference of the UK electorate. On the eve of the General Election, it took a number one régime troubleshooter like Dr Reid to proclaim seriously that all was well with Great Britain. 'The Union remains alive and well' he reassured *Scotsman* readers at the very end of 2000, just as the Election Campaign doors were being cranked open, '... [o]n the evidence of the last 12 months ... Britain has not died and is not gravely ill' (*The Scotsman*, 18 December 2000).[7]

This is the sort of thing one would normally expect to hear uttered by a bedside, in appropriately hushed tones. Yet here a suspicious tone of truculence adhered to his words as well – to which I will return below. At that time 'Doc' Reid was still Secretary of State for Scotland, and engaged in gunning down Separatists in the badlands, before his later posting to Northern Ireland.

---

7   Dr Reid's article claimed to be a review of *The State and the Nations: the First Year of Devolution in the United Kingdom*, edited by Robert Hazell (Imprint Academic 2000), but said remarkably little about it. This was just as well. Like his previous book *Constitutional Futures* (Clarendon Press 1999) Hazell's interim account was in truth extremely circumspect about the problems facing devolution, and highly critical of central failures and omissions.

Ill-fortune alone seems an inadequate explanation, either of this extraordinary collapse or of the weird 2001 election which was supposed to endorse it. Such unreality must surely derive from deeper causes. The historian and political scientist Timothy Garton Ash was nearer the mark in an *Independent* article, a few days after Watkins', headlined: 'The Old United Kingdom is Dead'. 'Is this the last *British* election?' he asked, meaning – 'The last time in which we can really speak of the politics of a single sovereign United Kingdom of Great Britain and Northern Ireland?' He cited the now lengthening list of European and Devolutionary reasons for such a fundamental doubt (to all of which I will return at more length below), and concluded: 'The old, centralised United Kingdom is dead. Long live the Federal Kingdom' (*Independent*, 28 May 2000).

Put his point in another way: the stage hypnotists and sullen audience of 7 June 2001 were compelled to go through their motions – the reproduction of a traditional Britain, crowned by Monarchy and attired in the feudality of Lordship, the reliquaries of caste and imperium, a domain of narrative cast in the familiar immemorial tones of stable repetition. They felt obliged to go on living as if Britain had not died, with troupes of hypnotists encouraging viewers in their suspension of disbelief. Institutions must reproduce themselves – including, perhaps most crucially of all, those of nation and state. But because actors and public alike continue to feel that the shades of Shakespeare, Milton and Edmund Burke are still in the building, it does not follow that they really are. They abandoned it some time ago, and what we are left with is not so much Britain as 'Britain' – the inverted-comma ex-Realm of Her Majesty. Dr Reid's 'Britain' has become another of Cipolla's pier-end performances – a miserable hypnotic stage-show, acceptable only to a public which, however modern in other ways, has yet to liberate itself *politically* from recollections of a former life.

In a single phrase, following Garton Ash: *Britain has actually ceased to exist*. It now belongs properly within its own tourist high-spot, Madame Tussaud's Famous Exhibition of Waxworks at Marylebone in London. The BBC's political correspondent Andrew Marr did bring out a book in 2000 called *The Day Britain Died*, but his speculative conclusions remained all too mild – in effect adding a serious question mark to his title. After the 2001 June election, the interrogation mark would seem quite superfluous. *Rigor mortis* was already advanced when Marr's book appeared, and even at that time remedy was there none. Blair started operations in 1997 with an impersonation of a glad, self-confident morning; four years later we find him racing to outpace the shade of night. All that has really happened in the time between is that (so to speak) Britain has remorselessly crumbled into vaudeville 'Britain', a realm of general impersonation and self-delusion, some of whose features I shall try to analyse below.

There is a crucial problem concealed within this transition from Britain (the '*ancien régime*') to present-day 'Britain', the realm of imposture. While old Britain – the United Kingdom – was quite well understood, its successor is not. The changeling has now been around for some time, but (of course) clutching on to the vestments of ancestral grandeur and world renown. These are now disguises. The old United Kingdom is dead all right, as Garton Ash surmises: dead, but far from buried. Rather, it seems to have joined the undead on Charon's ferry across the Styx, those unable quite to reach the realm of Hades. The ancient belief was that only those buried and mourned were allowed to attain that other shore. Otherwise they might drift indefinitely in limbo, unable either to forsake the living – so allowing *them* new life – or to enter the Underworld properly, passing the black watchdog Cerberus into the night of memory.

We understand the former polity a lot better than its miserable ghoul upon the ferry. The latter's rapid slide into insignificance is still being exorcised by loud claims of rebirth, and club-armchair ramblings about 'long-overdue modernisation'. However, Charon's heritage-site 'Britain' has now been long enough in existence (from, I would argue, the 1980s to the present) to evolve some depraved laws and customs of its own. These rites of passage into the afterlife are largely taken-for-granted extrapolations of past grandeur. In a theme park everything must of course be contrived to look and feel like history. But do we not know how such displays are managed by perfectly unhistorical criteria – number of visitors, reasons for visit, state of the toilets (and so on)? That the hallmarks of birthright and antecedence are constantly paraded is secondary: these are just part of the show, and themselves liable to quick 'modernisation', should numbers fall off, or if rumours continue to spread about the kitchens.

Thus Blairland is less the continuation of historical Britain than a degenerate parody of it – a substitute kept going only because it has, as yet, proved impossible to abolish the former state and system of political authority. Yet what the 2001 General Election may have done (inadvertently) is to establish a definitional landmark or bourne to this parodic or terminal phase. It did much more than unfairly re-elect a government. In retrospect, the sinking hearts and queasiness of the weeks before the 7th of June already anticipated that event. However, in the realm of the pseudo, pseudo-events can still be King. No longer historic, they may still be 'historic'. The bourne reached in this case was perhaps that of the historical British identity – the United Kingdom of the long era from 1688 to 1979. It was in the latter year (I will argue) that an unarrestable disintegration began, quite distinct from the longer cadences of 'decline' which had gone before. And what we know now, with much greater certainty than before 7 June 2001, is that no traveller will ever recross that bourne, or enter the historic realm of Britain again.

But also, I believe, it should have become clearer how urgent it now is to rid ourselves, once and for all, of the despicable look-alike which has usurped that realm. In the present short study I have chosen to emphasise those factors of past British identity and ideology that tend generally to be disregarded in commentary on elections and daily politics. That is, 'British identity' and its inseparable shadow, British *nationalism*, a taken-for-granted belief-system which informs most state attitudes, and still has an extensive penumbra of credibility among intellectuals linked to the metropolis or heartland, as well as some popular support (notably in Northern Ireland).

Under the present conditions of shrinkage and partial collapse, this form of nationality-politics is showing signs of become a campaign of unmitigated reaction. Redeeming the British day *faute de mieux* was one thing; saving and rejuvenating it *at all costs* may be turning into something else again – the game, and the spectacle, which was so recklessly promoted and aggravated by the General Election of 2001. It may not be easy to tell just when one turns into the other, but conservatism can become *reaction* when a state finds too many of its supports giving way simultaneously – when too much popular dislike accumulates, in ways that can no longer be easily suppressed or bought off.

This is why there are so many watchdogs about, straining at the leash to keep the population inside the Blair-Britain theme park for another five, ten or even twenty years. Tabloid-trained to mangle all attempts by inmates at taking over the asylum democratically, their mission has become to re-instil belief, to save the Crown and the House of Lords, to make sure everyone stays 'on message', and thus ensure that Great Britain will endure as a major ornament – even a leader – of the Globalised future. Blair's ministerial reshuffle immediately after the vote was aimed at extending this pack and building up its loyalty, under crude managerial slogans like 'Delivering Policies' and 'Government Cohesion'. 'Corporate populism' had become one interpretation of New Labour between 1997 and 2001.[8] But the post-June public relations outburst lacked even the

---

8   Anthony Barnett, 'The Dishonour', in *Prospect* magazine, January 2002.

shaky dignity of a corporation. It had much more affinity with an old-fashioned fairground where drunken fortune-tellers beguile passers-by, and hucksters strive to unload their stolen wares before the police arrive. Tim Garton Ash was somewhat ahead of events. As yet, the Old United Kingdom is only in its death-throes; and since the June 2001 election these have been growing even more malignant and protracted than before. Garton Ash is keen to see a more comely alternative emerging from the fogs ahead. But unfortunately, so I will argue, there is all too little sign or chance of any 'Federal Kingdom' emerging as a replacement.

2   CHANGELING KINGDOM

For some years now, and especially since February 1974, I have been oppressed by a sinister foreboding. We are living in the City of Destruction, a dying country in a dying civilization, and across the plain there is no wicket-gate offering a way of escape.

Quintin Hogg, Lord Hailsham,
The Dilemma of Democracy (Collins 1978), p. 15

How does New Labour's successor 'Britain' work? To avoid the inverted commas (incidentally) it may be simpler in what follows to use 'Ukania' as a shorthand, provided the reader notes that the reference is not primarily to Royal or archaic features of the neo-British system. It is the structure of the beast we need to observe, rather than its pelt and uniforms. The best man to enlighten us here is certainly Tony Blair himself. When he returned to report to the House of Commons on the European Nice Conference, in December 2000, these were his words:

It is possible, in our judgment, to fight Britain's corner, get the best out of Europe for Britain and exercise real authority and influence in Europe. That is as it should be. Britain is a world power. To stand aside from the key alliance – the European Union – right on our doorstep, is not advancing Britain's interests; it is betraying British interests. (*Hansard*, 11 December 2000, col. 351)

Greatness is all, in other words. For a world-power régime, being 'in Europe' is neither successor nor alternative to the past. It is simply one amongst other ways of remaining Great. The *Economist* put the same point rather well, in its first post-election issue:

Mr Blair is no 'declinist'. He believes that Britain can lead in Europe, not just take its place as a loyal member of the Union. Nor does he accept that leading in Europe implies weakening Britain's bond with America. He argues that Britain has a 'pivotal' role in world politics by virtue of its seat on the Security Council, closeness to the United States, membership of European Union and the G7, the credibility of its armed forces and the power of the English language. Mr Blair has relished cutting a dash on the world scene as an evangelist for his 'third way', saviour of Kosovo and the first Western leader to befriend Russia's President Putin. (*Economist*, 9 June 2001, pp. 37–8)

Thus, as Charles de Gaulle perceived long ago, a Euro-UK may exist alongside but will never be put *ahead* of the Special Relationship to the USA, the Commonwealth, over-valued Sterling, and the Crown. For Europe to become more important would somehow imply abandoning treasured stigmata: no longer being 'special' in that sense which means far more than 'different'. *Exceptionality* in this archaic sense is bestowed by either Providence or genes. To become European in the sense of *identifying* 'British interests' with European Union would therefore mean betrayal.

That is, it would imply downsizing, dilution, a retraction into the ordinariness of contemporary nationhood.

Late or terminal Britishness has in essence been one prolonged struggle against this fate. The Ukania of the 2001 election and funeral pyres is the result. In one sense, the struggle is being lost before our eyes. But unfortunately, the 2001 election will prolong that struggle too (as it was meant to do). It marked a farther circle of self-preserving 'continuity', in a country that has now moved well beyond 'decline'. Decline was the older, more genteel form of putrefaction which prevailed until the close of the 1970s. But from then on, a qualitatively distinct phase has taken over – the brazen simulacrum endured by all subjects of the Crown today.

I suggested above that academic and theoretical analysis has not yet adequately registered this important shift. That may be because it too tends to remain transfixed by the same tunnel-vision retrospect which affects Blair and his party. The (admittedly) long anterior time scale of Anglo-British statehood – from 1688 to the late twentieth century – has created dead generations who find themselves able to go on only by reconfiguring the present with overpowering templates drawn from the past. This is true above all at the level of state. The political apparatus which was originally a *sui generis* mode of advance (in the eighteenth century) has turned into a decaying and dumbed-down *impasse*. All the British nationalities have been confined within this cul-de-sac, and now periodically require electoral injections of fatality, 'continuity' and stable governance to keep them there.

While the origins of Ukanian downfall may be traced back far enough, to World War I and beyond, the acute phase we now know dates mainly from 1979. 'Declining Britain' had been happening for a century or so; but *parody*-Britain is a mere twenty-three years old. In that sense it is curiously like an unwillingly new nation. Only here, the novel 'identity' happens to consist in a ceaseless puppet-show of sere age, ever-unfolding legitimacy, and constant evocation of 1940, 'Our Finest Hour'. Mere habit and unshakeable nostalgia are not alone to blame. These are also orchestrated and brought out in repeated new productions, for quite real and pragmatic reasons. However, the latter are themselves unconfessable in theme-park terms. The heritage show bleats of 'identity', exemplary tribal customs, nostalgia, bygone glories and colours made bright once more. Without resorting to economic determinism, it must be said that straightforward economic motives remain prominent among the motives for such amazing persistence. The cash-nexus, the United Kingdom's venerable machinery of exchange and rake-off, still fits this form of state well enough to fuel its diminishing forward motion.

The year before Mrs Thatcher's ascent to power, former Tory Minister Lord Hailsham delivered an address on 'The Nation and the Constitution' which made a great impact. Most unusually for a political lecture in a fairly routine series, it is still remembered today. He argued that 'there has always been a danger inherent in our constitution that elective dictatorship would take over', and that this was now happening. He was thinking primarily about the Labour Party and Socialist Totalitarianism. Only six months later, a decisive slide began along just the lines he was predicting – but in the opposite political direction.

1979 was the year which saw a convulsion at the political level, the advent of a régime (not just an administration) much more self-consciously and radically committed to Redemption-politics than any before it. Mrs Thatcher said she would put the 'Great' back in Britain via a 'revolution', and she meant it. Wilson and Heath had certainly articulated some strands of the change back in the sixties and early seventies – the shifts which so worried Hailsham by 1978. But these were mere gutless men, paid-up subscribers to the Club of ruling-class decadence. They had compromised away the well-spring of national grandeur and left a woman to restore it.

As Dennis Kavanagh put it in a later study of Thatcherism, the foundations for her act were indeed already laid:

> The central issue in British politics has not been how to curb the elective dictatorship but how to capture it . . . Regardless of whether it is called a 'top-down' model or an elective dictatorship the formal concentration of political authority in Britain is remarkable.[9]

He enumerates its main 'top-down' features: a 'unitary system' averse to plural or contesting power; 'Sovereignty' wielded by one party (preferably with a large majority); total Treasury control and absence of a written constitution; and the conviction that extra-Parliamentary bodies are 'handmaidens', or compliant executives. It was impossible in 1986 (when Kavanagh was writing) to imagine how such a system could turn into today's parody of itself. At present, however – and more clearly since 7 June 2001 – we can now see how the 'tendencies' of Thatcherism were only precursors of a more decisive drama at the century's end.

The Winter of Discontent came immediately on the heels of Hailsham's lecture. Thatcher's New Conservatives had become rightly contemptuous of earlier failures, and of the wretched, stagnant 'consensus' they had fostered. Greatness was by then too visibly on the slide, and more

---

9   Kavanagh, *Thatcherism and British Politics: the End of Consensus?* (Oxford University Press 1986), p. 285. Professor Kavanagh has pursued his earlier theses more recently, to devastating effect. In a *Sunday Mail* article (24 September 1999) 'Why no one dares to argue with Napoleon Blair', he contended that phase-one Blairism was like a move from feudalism to Bonapartism. Even élite Cabinet government had almost vanished, and the true meaning of 'joined-up government' is just that – ultra-centralised dictatorial rule. 'For Bonaparte Blair there could yet be a Waterloo', he concludes sombrely. See also his book co-authored with Anthony Seldon, *The Powers Behind the Prime Minister: the Hidden Influence of No. 10* (HarperCollins 1999).

determined steps were needed to restore it. Thatcher believed that a violent plunge to the economic Right was the best formula, plus decisive shifts in the ideal climate of both state and society. Such was her 'entrepreneurial culture'. These shifts in outlook derived (Christopher Patten said at the time) from an abrupt rejection of the old-Labour idea of 'managing decline' as humanely as possible:

> That strategy fell to pieces in 1978–9. Mrs Thatcher took over committed to a very different view: that what governing Britain had to be about was arresting and reversing the decline . . . And that was clearly what she perceived as her mission.[10]

The mission coincided with a climatic change in Atlantic capitalism, and was soon seen as exemplary in that regard. But Thatcherism should not therefore be simply merged into this broader picture. A parochial British development fed into the general transformation, and was still capable of influencing it. Mrs Thatcher's domestic and social policy crusades were also part of that local narrative, succinctly described by Professor Jim Bulpitt in one of the most penetrating overviews of the period:

> The language of greatness was one which everybody could understand and which made the practice of mass democratic politics, once so feared, really rather easy; the language of national modernization, in contrast, strained not only people's intellects, but undermined the unity of the people under its accustomed leaders . . .[11]

---

10 Patten, as quoted in Hugo Young and Anne Sloman, *The Thatcher Phenomenon* (BBC Publications 1986), p. 139.

11 David Marquand and Anthony Seldon, *The Ideas That Shaped Post-War Britain* (Fontana 1996), Chapter 10, 'The European Question'. Bulpitt's earlier study quoted is *Territory and Power in the United Kingdom: an Interpretation* (Manchester University Press 1983).

'Language' here means 'assumptions' rather than stories: the inherited presuppositions of state authority, through which popular roots are maintained and a system can reproduce itself. Bulpitt had earlier written a magisterial account of this *ancien régime*, which he goes on to summarize in the 1996 essay. A year before Blair and New Labour came to office, he listed its features – worth quoting at length now, since as far as I know nobody since has done it better:

> First, a lethal electoral system based on single-member constituencies and simple majorities. Secondly, the persistence of a predominantly adversarial two-party system. Thirdly, the fact that both parties are dominated by temporary professional party leaders who for the duration give up most of their time and ambitions to managing their parties. Fourthly, the absence in Britain of any significant degree of institutional pluralism. In combination, these structural characteristics have produced party élites with common, initial, subsistence-level objectives, namely winning national office, avoiding too many problems while there, and getting re-elected. Any other objectives are jam on the bread . . . The absence of other significant centres of institutional power means that only national office is worth gaining: losing office – elections – means the political wilderness.

The overall judgement? According to Bulpitt, 'Court statecraft' remains the endemic milieu of British statehood, and is in a sense constitutive of the accompanying national identity: 'British governing is one long electoral campaign, albeit with different phases of intensity'. Remarkably little that happened in 2001 is not covered by this description of 1996. However, certain aspects of the system have grown more prominent since then.

Bulpitt did not employ the term, but the implication was clear (and inescapable today): *populism* was becoming the basis of the system. The 'top-down' or (in Hailsham's sense) 'dictatorial' structure adheres in the system, and not just in particular parties or their policies. In more expansive, outward-directed times, this may have been relatively tolerable. But when such a system fails, and contracts (both territorially and in influence) then its authority has to be reimposed by other methods. This means that the people have to be periodically readjusted to suit the system. In 1996, Bulpitt actually made the point more colourfully – British politicians will play 'dirty pool' to protect and advance their own interests. Dirty pool is simply the underbelly of 'the language of greatness'. In that sense the June 2001 General Election can be compared to an extended session of dirty pool.

At this point it is worth recalling another distinguished early analysis of the same thing, from a more defiantly left-wing angle: Stuart Hall's 'The Great Moving Right Show', first published in January 1979, four months before Thatcher was voted in.[12] Hall's account was based primarily on ideological and cultural factors, and drew inspiration from Gramsci's *Prison Notebooks*. It was pointed out there that 'crises' are not (or not necessarily) brief episodes of high drama, but can 'last for decades'. During such periods it grows impossible merely to 'conserve' a *status quo* or old régime, however treasured and sacrosanct. The political Right has to take the offensive, and in a sense rival the Left by becoming more self-consciously 'formative'. This situation poses the severest problems of readjustment for the Left. Confronted by right-wing initiatives apparently more 'radical' (or even 'revolutionary') than those of a Left now fossilised and over-institutional, the latter may even go under altogether (as of course happened in 1920s Italy). There, Socialists and Communists were

---

12 *Marxism Today* (January 1979), later reproduced in *The Politics of Thatcherism* (Lawrence & Wishart 1983) edited by Stuart Hall and Martin Jacques, Section I, 'The Background'. References here are to the book version.

brutally shown they had no monopoly of novelty or reform, or of class and popular support.

Hall's analysis perceived something analogous under way in the United Kingdom, where Thatcherite Conservatism had also succeeded in building a form of authoritarian populism. She had translated the theoretical ideology of Free Trade and anti-state individualism into a new 'populist idiom' – an alternative ethic to that of the 'caring society'. Hall was writing in the 1978–79 'Winter of Discontent', which millions of voters would now do anything to avoid in future. In fact they rushed to embrace a weird fusion of Tory traditional values and *laisser-faire*, which at least had the merit of promising a new start: '[Mrs Thatcher] constructed the people into a populist political subject: *with*, not against the power-bloc: in alliance with new political forces in a great national crusade to "make Britain 'Great' once more . . ."'[13] Gramsci had a word for this too: *il trasformismo* – the appropriation of previously hostile or dissident ideas or impulses into 'a new political configuration' which carried them in a different direction. But what Hall could not know then was that 'transformism' would go on to enjoy much greater success and longer life in Britain than it had done in Italy. In 1979 'The Great Moving Right Show' pleaded for a reformed and modernized Left. By the 1990s the latter had indeed come to exist, but only to reappropriate the 'populist idiom' of Thatcherism. Dirty pool was to become both chronic and systematic. The former Left then embarked upon *its own* national crusade of restored Greatness, powered by even less restrained ideological and cultural means, and by increasingly plebiscitary elections. 'Greatness' proved insatiable. It has devoured all its children one after another.

The 'climatic change' I mentioned earlier has been the necessary

---

13 Hall and Jacques, *op. cit.*, pp. 30–31, 'The Repertoire of Thatcherism'.

condition for both the Moving Right and the 'Moving Left' show which followed. However, the *sufficient* conditions for such a degeneration are of course more than that. They must lie in the specific motives and trajectory of the UK state – a history 'special' indeed, if not quite in the self-congratulatory sense so dear to the Whig Interpretation of History.

Many real changes did come about from Mrs Thatcher's efforts, but restored grandeur was not among them. After her overthrow in 1990, the Kingdom lapsed into the pothole of 'Black Wednesday' (the currency collapse of 1992) and then into John Major's half-decade of miasmic torpor. After which a further 'revolution' was plainly required. It could now come only from the Left, and duly did so in 1997. The 'Blairism' that followed sought to benefit from Thatcherism's economic convulsion, while orchestrating an even more startling shift of *mentalités* under the assorted banners of the Third Way. In the British version, this was a speculative navigational chart intended to reconcile the Enterprise Culture with the remains of Welfarism – but always within the inherited hulk of the Constitution.[14] Though naturally broadcast as a set of signposts for the Firmament, Blair's nebulous concoction rested upon the shakiest feet in the old-fashioned 'West'. It was a way of keeping the Westminster Monarchy and State going (envy of the world, etc.). Britain and its

---

14 The antecedents of Third-Wayism are longer and more ambiguous than the enthusiasts of 1997 realised. Some have traced it back to Australia – see Chris Pierson and Francis Castles, 'Australian Antecedents of the Third Way', on www.essex.ac.uk/ecpr/. But in Zeev Sternhell's *Neither Right nor Left* (University of California Press 1986) there is an interesting analysis of efforts to 'transcend' the outmoded right–left polarity in 1930s France. This paved the way for Pétain in 1940. Those wishing an updated horoscope on Third Way questions will find it in the *New Statesman*'s post-election issue: 'Just Carry on Being New' (sic) by Anthony Giddens. The most entertaining reflections on the Third Way recently have been those of Roy Hattersley, in *Granta* magazine No. 71 (2001) – 'In Search of the Third Way'.

accompanying Greatness were to experience giddy regrowth under a second magician's spell. Right-wing authoritarian populism was thus quite easily transformed into its Left-wing equivalent, an alternative (and soon almost indistinguishable) flight-path to maintain pivotal or 'world' power.

In disillusionment, many on the Left have fallen back upon a 'no difference' interpretation of such continuities. But it is important to avoid this too. The *content* of governance in Redemption-Britain is indeed pretty much the same. But government is more than policies: it is the embodiment across time of a state, and of its accompanying identity. And here, both chronology and cumulative effects (including unintended effects) are also vital. For example, one vital difference the 1997 Redemption-spasm has brought is confirmation of Britain's terminal phase *as a system*. In 1979 Lord Hailsham was really concerned about one government or Premier becoming dictatorial (most likely a Socialist). He did not envisage Conservatism too as part of the darkling plain stretching to the horizon, where ever less choice might be permitted between competing dictatorships, and where watchdogs would pounce on anyone approaching a wicket-gate.

More than one party or government is needed to speak of a 'régime' – but the latter quite clearly emerged in Blair's first term in office, and has now been officiously blessed by his steam-roller election of 2001. This is a 'Britain' (as I suggested earlier) with distinctive rules and tendencies of its own. At a certain point, so many modifications or shifts in any longer *durée* can constitute a duration or 'phase' of their own. Whether long- or short-lived, these rules are most likely to be corrupted (or 'modernised') descendants of famous ancestors. They are the 'undead' of historical British Constitutionalism, as it were, failing to give up their hold over a soil and people which should long ago have been freed of them. 2001 also showed that the deadly grip remains a fairly strong one. It is that of a system designed to stifle the emergence of rival power-structures, and it still does so effectively.

The tendencies now so clearly on show were first intuitively diagnosed by Robin Blackburn in a *New Left Review* article, 'Blair's Velvet Revolution' (NLR 1/223, May–June 1997). Writing about New Labour's recent poll triumph, he questioned 'a disquieting strain in New Labour politics that could easily curdle the hopes now aroused, namely its personalism and authoritarianism'. Even then, the 'demagogic proclivity' of the Leadership appeared strong enough to throw doubt upon Blair's 'credibility as a force for democratization'. Was there not in fact 'a tiny but not totally insignificant resemblance to be found between Britain's new Prime Minister ... and France's new President in 1848?' Louis Napoleon rose to power representing a weakened Republican Left, after the turmoil following the repression of the 1848 revolution; Blair's ascent came after the long subjugation of the Thatcher and Major years, and the 'trouncing of organized labour'. Were not both of them populists, glib rhetoricians and compromisers, with a taste for plebiscitary power? Napoleon also brandished an equivalent to the Third Way of 1997, with his notions of marrying Liberalism and Saint-Simonian Socialism. And four years later he was Emperor of France as 'Napoleon the Third'. 'So we may hope that it will never be necessary to write on "The 18th Brumaire of Tony Blair"', concluded Blackburn.

The author's perceptiveness must be admired. But his hope was ill-founded. Four years on, after the General Election of June 2001, this is exactly what everybody was writing about, in one way or another. I have already given some examples, and there are plenty more to follow. The British post-1979 system has allowed New Labour to make the transition without bloodshed or a *coup d'état*. But only because it was already pre-disposed to abuse of this kind. As Hailsham feared, 'a dying country' of elective dictatorship was collapsing along the fault-lines of populism and (as Blackburn put it) 'the repressive reflex'.

Like Thatcherism before it, Blairism naturally lays claim to an essential continuity with the 1688–1979 United Kingdom. At one level of perception, the claim can be all too easily justified. As we saw, the uniforms and mementoes of former times continue to litter London, and Heritage displays are kept running at Buckingham Palace and Windsor, as well as in the Palace of Westminster. Britain goes on asserting its 'presence' in the skies of the Balkans and the Middle East, and retains both a Nuclear Deterrent and its Security Council seat. The institutions of Great Britain go on reproducing themselves through another set of bearers or agents (or victims), as indeed they are bound to do until defeated, seriously reformed or just abandoned. Their crucial embodiment is the customary axis between the Royal Palaces of Westminster and Buckingham, the unwritten Crown Constitution. Hailsham perceived that as the source of the deterioration all right. But after 1979 he was deluded enough to think Thatcher would put things right. Instead (with some help from the noble Lord himself) what she did was to inaugurate a genuinely unique *two-party* 'dictatorship': a conjoined and bipartisan 'soft totalitarianism' whose foundations still seemed strong enough not (or not yet) to require a single party in unremitting charge, or a 'dictator for life'.

In 1979 (one should recall) there were already some examples of *one-party* crypto-dictatorships. That is, of long-term régimes where elections served primarily as plebiscites, or renewal-mandates like Thatcher's in 1987, or Blair's in 2001. Professor T.J. Pempel analysed these in his comparative study *Uncommon Democracies: The One Party Dominant Régimes* (1990). Under Cold War conditions, he pointed out that 'permanent or semi-permanent governance by a single party, alone or at the heart of a coalition, provides a potentially extreme case of one party that is the glue in a political régime'. Such régimes are capable of constructing a 'virtuous cycle' which then maintains them in power over decades, even many decades.

Such virtuous cycles are most evident in the four countries that are the focal point here – Sweden, Israel, Japan, and Italy. They all show to varying degrees the combined interaction of dominance in socioeconomic mobilization, intraparty bargaining, public policy, and longevity.[15]

All these régimes ended, in fact, and in different ways have returned to more authentic parliamentary politics. In the case of Italy the régime endured for forty years, during which time innumerable elections and minor constitutional reforms served mainly to preserve the rock-like hegemony of Christian Democracy. It collapsed not long after Pempel's book was published, plunging the country into a far more chaotic democracy than anything that *Democrazia Cristiana* had feared during its geological epoch of hegemony. Like Hailsham, it had dreaded the Left; a few years later, it too would be swamped by a neo-liberal (or 'Thatcherite') demagogue of the Right.

At times in the later 1980s it did look as if 'Thatcherism' might be coalescing into a stranglehold like those antecedents. Many people felt that she or her system might somehow last for ever, or that (in Stuart Hall's terms) the 'moving-right show' might simply develop into the only show in town.[16] But there was one very significant difference. The 'uncommon democracies' discussed in Pempel's book had one thing in common: 'All cases of one-party dominance (occurred) *under variants of proportional representation*

---

15 T.J. Pempel, *Uncommon Democracies: The One Party Dominant Régimes* (Cornell University Press 1990), 'Introduction', pp. 15–16.

16 They included the author, who was unwise enough to publish an essay on the subject in *New Left Review* in 1993 (July–August, First Series, No. 200, 'The Sold Survivor', pp. 41–7). I suggested that Britain might end up as one of Pempel's semi-eternal right-wing one-party structures, thus underestimating the capacity of Labourism to embrace the UK variant of *trasformismo*, in accordance with a deeper impulse of state continuity.

and electoral systems that foster multipartism', he wrote. Though the systems varied greatly, and democratic sclerosis cannot be blamed on one factor alone, he concluded that 'multipartism is certainly a precondition for the emergence of one-party dominance'. The United Kingdom, however, had a system which always acted powerfully *against* multipartism.

In Ukania, as in the United States, the 'system' was linked to an exceptionally powerful *national* framework. In the USA this is of course the Greatest Constitution in the world, as set down by the late-eighteenth-century founding fathers, sworn to every morning in schools, displayed in a sacred flag-emblem, and carried massively onward by a cultural tradition ranging from neo-classic architecture to *The Simpsons*. In Great Britain, an analogous but *unwritten* Constitution goes back even longer (to 1688 and 1707), and endured until the 1970s with equivalent effects and success. Being unwritten, its historical logic was different: quieter, more informal and (above all) embodied by *a class* rather than through the rhetorically undifferentiated citizenship of Americans.

Differences notwithstanding, both systems have shared another feature: a sustaining religiosity felt to be indispensable both as 'social glue' and as the justification of national outreach, or 'standing' in the world. American piety is more ostentatious than the British kind: the glue has to be visible, and publicly advertised as the 'private' dimension of Americanness. However, Linda Colley showed in her *Britons* (1992) that in a broad sense 'Protestantism lay at the core of British national identity . . . The Protestant worldview which allowed so many Britons to see themselves as a distinct and chosen people persisted long after the Battle of Waterloo'. (pp. 368–9).

As a matter of fact, we saw it persisting at least until 8 May 2001, the day upon which Tony Blair announced the date of his coming election. Instead of a straightforward message (conventionally delivered at Downing Street) Blair chose to go to a church school in South London to launch his campaign. It was, as Joe Klein noted in the *New Yorker* (4 June 2001), an 'American-style' publicity stunt, staged in the school Assembly hour associated with God and musing upon Higher Things. The Prime Minister was depicted by most papers with a stained-glass window behind him, and caustically dismissed as a preacher delivering a sermon on times past and to come (which was exactly what he was doing). Klein reported the 'universal disgust' at this stunt, even among Labour's friends. It stank of spin-doctoring and American influence.

The diagnosis was no doubt right but (one suspects) rather misplaced. PR alone was not to blame here. Blair's religiosity is deeper, and aligned with the tradition Colley has analysed. It represents what Arthur Marwick has called 'the Anglican compromise' once felt as essential to the old style of class rule, a motif fusing together state and private conviction, and appealing strongly (if nowadays subliminally) to an important ingredient of Britishness.[17] It evokes the identity-reflex Marwick delineated as follows:

> The British upper class, though poorly educated compared with its European counterparts, has continuously fostered the notion, unfortunately very readily accepted throughout society, that British ways are not just best, but eternal. In tacit collaboration with the major unions this class encouraged belief in the divine right of the big battalions, at the expense of genuine innovation and enterprise.[18]

---

17 It makes no difference that Blair is coy about this when questioned directly. In a *Sunday Times* profile published at the same time (3 June), he is recorded as saying: 'God? Well it's a help, isn't it? I don't really want to talk about it because it's always misunderstood by people, they try to capitalize on your religious faith.' He then recounts how he desires above all to appear 'just another bloke . . . not something special'. The evangelical overture to the electoral campaign was of course aimed precisely at the sensibility of such 'ordinary British blokes'.

18 Arthur Marwick, *Britain in Our Century: Images and Controversies* (Thames & Hudson 1984), Chapter 10, 'Britain Today: New Course, or Same But Worse?', pp. 212–13.

As I shall argue later, this remains a crucial element in 'Blairism' – and almost certainly for the understanding of the supposedly 'enigmatic' personality of the Prime Minister himself.

In short, two-party or alternate-team electoral dictatorship expresses an unusually strong state-*nation* identity, with an associated form of nationalism resilient enough to encompass such 'transformism' – *at least for a time*. Pempel observed how prolonged one-party rule has generally arisen in response to crisis. A party which 'saves the state' can then deploy its prestige and assets over long periods, while carefully preserving the forms of democracy. But British redemptionism is more broadly based than this. No one party can be credited with rescuing the United Kingdom from decline. Instead, the Conservative Party launched a system-renewal which proved both transformable and transmissible – capable of turning into a 'régime' in fact.

But there is a troubling downside to this, which sums up a good deal of contemporary Britain: a *system* may not be alterable or replaceable in the way that one-party hegemony usually has been. Pempel observes how 'one-party dominance' depended on 'multipartism' and proportional representation. And as both his own account and subsequent events have demonstrated, multipartism *was also the longer-term solution* to the elements of threat and suffocation inherent in single-party rule. When the causative crisis is over (or is replaced by another) then the system can revert to the 'norms' prescribed by written constitutions and expressed in some kind of proportional representation. In the United Kingdom this is manifestly not the case.

Remember Kavanagh's list of characteristics or 'top-down' features: 'a "unitary system" averse to plural or contesting power; "Sovereignty" wielded by one party (preferably with a large majority); total Treasury control and absence of a written constitution; and the conviction that extra-Parliamentary bodies are "handmaidens", or compliant executives.'

And, always in final system-command – '*a lethal electoral system* based on single-member constituencies and simple majorities'. In other words, such a broader authority contains all 'permissible' alternatives within itself, and renders it extremely difficult to change the system from within. A specious pretence of 'flexibility' and evolving openness conceals rigid underlying determination to stay the same: 'British', that is, 'pivotal', 'cutting a dash' (and so on). However shrunk and corrupted, *the* system remains consecrated by such entrenched national parameters, and by the semi-sacred identity narrative that has always justified them. The 'Great' goes on belonging in 'Britain', in Marwick's sense, a symbol of guaranteed eternity.

Of course few in the wider world are now deceived. They more readily perceive a parodic realm, even a caricatural one. Especially since June 2001, impersonation can no longer be confused with real continuity. State institutional life may perpetuate itself, as (for example) it did after Marshall Tito's passing in Yugoslavia, or during the reign of Gorbachev in the USSR; but neither the masses nor the outside world are obliged to take it seriously. 'Britain' is simultaneously the heir to and the absolute betrayer of its past and traditions. Unable to reform itself decisively enough, the United Kingdom state has in turn fallen back into a kind of institutional palsy, *rigor mortis* disguised as resolution, and fixed-grin happiness with a resplendent past.

Yet decomposition cannot really be kept at bay. In one way or another, the chemistry of decay is bound to creep in and replace or falsify the principles of an over-celebrated traditionalism. Thus Dorian Gray-Blair gazes every day into his reconstructed portrait of unaltering youth, the rejuvenation and prolongation of a legendary past; but with each new shock or revelation, the truth shows through, like some subjacent and remorseless fungus. The process now seems certain to continue for another five, ten or more years – at which point, late-British theatre decrees that another (preferably from 'the other party') will take up his station at the mirror. 'Events, dear boy, events!' Prime Minister Harold Macmillan said of the

1960s world, even then betraying him, towards the end of what we can now perceive as the true *ancien régime* of Britain. Not by chance have these become perhaps the most commonly quoted words of the after-life polity which he was to leave behind. The inescapable unreality of the 2001 election and the Blairite *régime* is that of a *revenant* existence, still clinging to life on this side of the grave.[19]

3   MYTHOLOGICAL GREATNESS

Indirect Rule flourished in the Empire as a governing ethos which, with its emphasis on character rather than training, its primitive notions of justice, its exaltation of the autonomous agent unhindered by outside control, its demand for loving awe from the governed, was unmistakably the product of an earlier age. The persistence of this primitive conception of the nature of authority . . . was not without its consequences for the future of the Empire . . .

Kathryn Tidrick, *Empire and the English Character*
(I.B. Tauris 1992), p. 221

---

19 For a decreasing number of readers, some sense of *déja vu* will be inevitable at this point. The underlying argument advanced has a forty-year history stretching from the early years of the *New Left Review* down to the present: that is, from Perry Anderson's 'Origins of the Present Crisis' down to and now through the 'crisis' itself. Once given hedge-baptism as 'the Nairn–Anderson theses' about the anachronism and decline of Great Britain, that gloomy prognosis of so many decades ago is now being far eclipsed by events themselves. My argument here unavoidably uses absurd compressions and elipses of what was a long-drawn-out affair, for which I must apologise. Readers anxious to catch up with the fuller history will find the greater part of it in Perry Anderson's collection *English Questions* (Verso 1990), especially the Introduction's concise narration of the 1960s, and of the background to his 'Origins of the Present Crisis' in *New Left Review*.

Some more historical perspective is needed, simply to track the great (and continuing) 1979 shift. Until well after World War II, all things genuinely British were a fusion of empire and class. Between Victoria's accession in 1837 and the victory of 1945, the UK was ruled by a single, hereditary élite complex enough to support different political parties.[20] This one-class state achieved its astonishing domestic dominance primarily by a deployment of *external* resources and relationships.

This is what really underlies the unshakeable obsession with being a 'world power'. The fact is that 'greatness', international weight and special influence, were never secondary to Anglo-Britain's characteristic state. They were not apprehended as a mere addition to Britain's political arsenal – like a bonus or a stroke of good luck that might eventually be put aside. Rather, for around two hundred years they were considered essential for economy and state alike, and a class structure came to be crystallised around them. They engendered a unique form of rule, which for long embraced both the formal state and many features of civil society. That configuration of outreach has always been a key ingredient of 'Britishness', more like an organic extension of the English identity than simply another layer of it, or one of its options.

'Outreach' is both much less and much more than colonial, or even 'informal', overseas empire. In the British case, it denotes something like an imperium of commerce, which for a time comprised foreign territories and 'subject peoples', but was at no point wholly dependent upon

20 The most definitive study of the matrix of Anglo-British statehood is Ellis Wasson's *Born to Rule: British Political Elites* (Sutton Publishing 2000). He shows how up until late in the nineteenth century 'the governing classes of the three kingdoms and principality in the British Isles *never amounted in total to much more than about 2,500*' (p. 159).

these. And when they vanished between the 1940s and the 1970s, the imperium-core not only survived but flourished. That is, the City or exchange-centre of London retained or even expanded its function in the Cold War era.[21]

What did decline terminally over the same period was the *industrial* sector of British capitalism – often wrongly regarded as the most important part, or even as the basis, of the United Kingdom economy. Karl Marx and many successors believed that the earlier forms of commerce and 'trading empire' were paving the way for the ascendancy of industry and science-based technology – was this not what made England the leading, archetypal society of the nineteenth century? But in fact the 'industrial revolution' developed far more vigorously in those other countries which followed its example: Germany, the United States and then (in the twentieth century) dozens of others. Britain had a key function in the genesis of industrialism; but it was never archetypal. The extractive and manufacturing industries of its matrix – Northern England, Lowland Scotland and South Wales – did not long survive the end of British colonialism. In fact their final shrinkage or eclipse has been the accompaniment (and partly the explanation) of New Labour's parodic 'Britain'.

'British society as a whole is not "retarded" or "advanced"', wrote Geoffrey Ingham in his *Capitalism Divided* (1984), 'it constitutes a unique

---

21 In a magisterial overview of Europe, sociologist Göran Therborn points out that 'globalisation' has been quite good for London: 'In the gigantic area of foreign currency trading, London has recently reinforced its standing as *the* centre of the world'. See *The Question of Europe* (Verso 1997), edited by Perry Anderson and Peter Gowan, pp. 370–71. Therborn adds a characteristic comment, quite important for grasping the ideological undergrowth of the Blair–Brown metropolis: 'Financial markets . . . are generally manned by highly paid young males, to whom social issues are as alien as the other side of the moon' (p. 366).

case of one in which international commercial capitalism has been dominant, and has had a determinant impact on its class and institutional structure'. Later on Ingham points out how Marxism and the voices of British industrialism colluded in ignorance of that impact. They took the Industrial Revolution too seriously, imagining that the UK must be fated to an exemplary manufacturing future – and must therefore develop an appropriate state to serve it. Their blueprint called for a technocratic polity something like post-World War II France: an energising bureaucracy, with a public sector leading 'productive' capital to feats of dominance. Hence these critics, according to Ingham:

> failed to consider in full (that) these originally 'pre-industrial' elements would be required in an expanded form by the world system, and that Britain was prepared to maintain them in positions of relative dominance. It is international commerce and banking which . . . have determined the trajectory of British capitalist development as a national economy within the world capitalist system.[22]

This meant that the 'archaic' (or pre-industrial) state form that originated in 1688 and 1707 remained fairly compatible with social modernisation. It represented an oligarchy that rode the storm of industrial development quite well, because of the alternative economy to which it was linked. And one way of doing that was by the defence (or where necessary the re-creation) of 'archaism' and its associated ideas and institutions. The Monarchy, aristocracy, the House of Lords, the Public (that is, private) school system, literary nostalgia and all the other relics listed by so many

---

22 Geoffrey Ingham, *Capitalism Divided? The City and Industry in British Social Development* (Schocken Books 1984), pp. 6 and 89.

modernist and left-wing critiques also had the function of conserving that alternative. They offered a 'national-popular' identity whose object was less to obstruct industry than to promote and stiffen commercial and financial outreach. Thus 'Tradition' preserved a system consecrated by wealth, as well as by romantic mythology and pastoral nonsense.

One key consequence was to be a certain deformation of the national identity in question. This system was 'British', rather than 'English', for a variety of important reasons. 1707 (the Union with Scotland) and 1800 (Union with Ireland) were of course important factors in themselves. But also, the exchange-imperium of the City depended primarily upon *one part* of territorial England, rather than upon the whole. W.D. Rubinstein has written most eloquently on this theme in his study of culture and decline in modern Britain: 'London's place in the structure of British life was and perhaps still is unique among comparable countries: perhaps nowhere else is the size, function and centrality of the Metropolis equal to that of London, a fact which has been true since Elizabethan times.'[23] The unitarism of the British polity always reflected this, as well as the homogeneous lifestyle and formation of the patriciate. London and its environs were the latter's natural nexus: simultaneously the 'homeland' of a caste and the base of a commercial, outreaching economy dependent on trade rather than industry.

Thus the modern British state has never relied upon geographical or territorial England. This is why, during the long period over which free-trade imperialism and the Royal Navy were built up, 'Little England' turned into a barred road – a left-over backyard, primarily a resort of the soured and disgruntled. Whether as boast or (more often) as sneer, the

---

23 W.D. Rubinstein, 'Elites and the Evolution of the Economy', *Capitalism, Culture and Decline in Britain, 1750–1990* (Routledge 1993) p. 158.

phrase came to denote territorial (and industrial) England, the 'home country' minus its colonies, and without its overseas role as global gendarme. That role is of course the ancestor of the pivotal '*Pax Britannica*' which Tony Blair has lamely revived in the aftermath of the terror-attacks of 11 September 2001. 'Little England' tended to be used dismissively or defensively. The commercial and landed Establishment perceived the idea as wilful negativism, indeed practically a form of self-immolation. Did it not amount to belittlement of that grander Englishness which had so naturally extended outwards and embraced the whole world? *Their* 'national interest' was, on the contrary, forever wedded to being 'pivotal' and outward-looking in just that sense. 'Identity' came to be permanently defined by that grander perspective.

Such expansive redefinition later assumed both a right-wing coloration (racism) and a left-wing one (universalism or internationalism). But both of these rested on a denial of core identity. The previous English state of late-mediaeval times, a product of Anglo-Saxon and Norman conquests, became 'greater' England in two phases: through subordination – but not assimilation – of the archipelago, then (more decisively) by overseas commercial and colonial development from the seventeenth century onwards. Hence the twenty-first-century paradox: a 'nation' accounting for over 80 per cent of the population of 'the Isles', but with almost no separate *modern* political identity of its own. The great English Revolution of 1640 to 1688 founded a state which endures to this day; but this state could not help coinciding in formation, development and self-image with the successful outreach of a commercial, and then a colonial, imperium. It was condemned by its own developmental path to be 'great'. This is why 'greatness' (inseparable from Britain, etc.) is no mere moral or aspirational term. It has also reflected a structural fate, a former advantage become a crippling retrospect.

Greatness in that sense has as its opposite *nothingness*. The poignancy of present-day British collapse lies partly in this resultant question mark. In 2001 'England' has to be reinvented, not just belatedly but in a sense *posthumously*. And something increasingly uncomfortable comes not far behind: preventing a littler England from returning in this way may help, it may indeed be essential, to *save Britain*. If that is so, then Englishness would obviously be best kept for Christmas cards (as Scottishness used to be, until rashly returned to political existence in 1997). Ukania believed itself secure in devolving some power to the little nations of its periphery: but Devolution to a potentially little England represents another scale of risk altogether.

This uniquely false consciousness has become an important stumbling-block for the twenty-first-century Isles. What was so useful in the construction of an extended hegemony has turned into a fatal flaw in its deconstruction. While there are many ways of analysing both the power-structure and its present *impasse*, what must concern us here are its political forms. There is one striking fact which demonstrated the power and nature of the resultant hegemony. Between 1915 and 1945, the long world crisis – wars, fascism, slump and the fall of most other imperial systems – was confronted in Britain primarily by 'National Governments'. Under these political coalitions, the British ruling class buried its many differences 'for the duration' (which turned out to be thirty years long).

Such emergency-period unity was one of the true precedents for the Thatcher and Blair régimes of post-1979 Redemption. End-game Britishness has found little abroad to emulate, apart from garbled mis-readings of the USA. But it did have this suggestive ancestral phase within its own history, during the generation from the Lloyd-George coalition in World War I, up to Churchill's all-party government of 1940–45. In short, parody-Britain may be the nearest the state can now get to 'National Government' in that fabled and effective sense. Of course it must do so under conditions in which many of the original supports for the old mode of governance have disappeared, like social deference and Empire.

Subsequently, many liberal and left-wing commentators have sought to dismiss the earlier 1915–45 period as one when the Conservative Party ruled 'in disguise'. However, they overlook how convincing the camouflage seemed to their own political forebears. No litany of 'betrayal' and 'sell-out' can account for the success of such co-option, or for its culmination in Churchill's 1940 leadership.[24] The adversarial representative system proved 'retractable' under sufficient pressure. And the device only worked because the social divisions of a notorious caste-like society were less decisive than the external constraints of empire and commerce. It was in the later part of this era that the Labour Party graduated into that original 'Establishment'; by the fifties it had completely absorbed most of its world-view. Such assumptions are extraordinarily tenacious – as 'Blairism' was to demonstrate, right up to the present. Once institutionally embedded, they are like the 'deep grammar' of state-life, underlying the surface eddies of policies and events.

Of course it does not follow that the *reality* of that period's statehood still prevails today. On the contrary, from the 1950s onwards – just as Labourism was becoming finally and acceptably British – the very foundations of the British *Weltanschauung* had begun to change implacably. Externally, the territorial extensions of a commercial empire disappeared, leaving behind only its core in the City of London money and commodity

---

24 The most illuminating account to appear is John Lukacs's *Five Days in London, May 1940* (Yale University Press 2000), an hour-by-hour description of how Winston Churchill remade the 1940 National Government at the time of the Dunkirk defeat. His reconstruction of the deeper grammar of Britishness was extremely effective, and has echoed consistently through the feebler ideological constructions of both Thatcherism and Blairism.

markets. As we have seen, this did prove very durable, and adaptable. Most of late-Britain's unceasing régime-slogans about its ineffable Constitution, 'flexibility', 'adaptability', 'realism' (and so on), apply much better to the radioactive element at its heart, the City of London, than they ever did to the institutions of Westminster.[25] However, the new prosperity of the fifties and sixties did undermine the social buttresses of the preceding *régime*: 'deference', and the stagnant class corporatism of the imperial era. From then onwards, the state and identity configuration of 'Britishness' would have to perpetuate itself minus much of the original 'navel' which had both fed and justified its being – that is, the conjuncture of naval empire and a land-based élite at home.

In these circumstances, the patriciate decayed from the sixties onwards, and lost its old nerve. By 1979 it had lost its socio-cultural grip. There were quite a few grandees in Thatcher's first Cabinet, but the *class* of Churchill was gone. Of those remaining, a few joined the opposition, some became centurions of the 'revolution' (like Nicholas Ridley and William Whitelaw), while the rest swallowed their pride as Heritage or fashion icons. Astonishingly, one of them did re-materialise as a contender for leadership of the Conservative Party after Hague's resignation on 8 June 2001: Michael, Earl of Ancram. But this can probably be put down to out-right despair at the wretched prospect of farther years in the desert. Otherwise, the heirs of those who bestrode the globe are today defenders

---

25 Coincidentally, the day I was writing this, the *Observer* business pages carried a big headline: 'City Set for Huge Expansion'. 'The Corporation of London is planning a dramatic expansion of the Square Mile to cope with huge demand from international banks and to maintain the City's place as Europe's top financial centre . . .' (3 June 2001). 'The move is supported by London Mayor Ken Livingstone', the article concludes, 'as long as the economic benefits percolate through to deprived boroughs'. In Rubinstein's terms, one could be in 1801 as easily as in 2001.

of 'the Countryside', notably fox-hunting. What the sociological changes of the 1960s had begun, Margaret Thatcher's lower-middle-class crusade then finished off during the 1980s.

This meant that the previous political formula was ruled out. The world of outreach greatness had not ceased to be essential: 'who we are', the British way as distinct from that of the land-bound Continental armadillos. To this day there is felt to be no escape from that. But because its domestic basis was breaking up, farther emergency and decline could no longer be dealt with by the device of 'National Government'. The parties were now quite unable to 'come together' in that old way – a tragedy often ascribed to the pernicious side-effects of an 'age of affluence', self-indulgence and the decline of 'patriotism'. Edmund Burke's 'great oaks that shade a country' were now turning into tourist attractions for those that 'creep on the ground' – those subjects who 'perish without season and leave no trace behind us'.[26]

A resentful sort of rebelliousness was gnawing at the oak tree roots, disabling the linked stabilities of class and Crown. Dismissed as vulgar, or even 'yobbish', by an élite still patrician in its attitudes, this fairly ordinary individualism was even then building up a reservoir of populist resentment – alienation misconstrued (most often) as damnable modernity and heedless hedonism. This grew steadily more salient after 1979, and found notable manifestation in the year or so before the June 2001 election. And yet, over this entire generational period, the longer and more fundamental 'emergency' of Britain's fall into insignificance never ceased to intensify. A state and culture now increasingly anachronistic were forced, therefore, towards new stratagems of survival.

---

26 *The Portable Edmund Burke*, edited by Isaac Kramnick (Viking 1999), 'Introduction', p. xiii.

This is surely why, as crisis deepened, each party has from the seventies onwards sought *to become the state and nation* – that is, to keep up or even reconstitute British Unionism by astute will-power, theatrical coups and the deployment of ever more capillary forms of control. These include the opinion-massage linked to the 'control freaks' described by Nicholas Jones in his book of the same name, and the informal 'task forces' listed by Tony Barker in his *Ruling by Task Force* (1999). Under these circumstances, what theorists use to call the 'autonomy of politics' has become the pretention of its would-be omnipotence. [27]

'Autonomy' had been the belated acknowledgement by left-wing (notably Marxist) sociology that statehood is not 'determined' by a machinery of economic forces. It has its own sources, influence and (therefore) 'laws' which mould economic patterns as well as expressing them. But in most contemporary societies (including those singled out by T.J. Pempel, discussed above) such transactions go on via written constitutions

---

27 See *The Control Freaks: How New Labour Gets its Own Way* (Politico's 2001) by Nicholas Jones and *Ruling by Task Force: Politico's Guide to Labour's New Elite*, by Tony Barker with Iain Byrne and Aanjuli Veall (Politico's in association with Democratic Audit 1999, Preface by Trevor Smith). Both these studies, but particularly the second, give a vivid idea of the spider's web (or 'network') through which the synthesised patriciate of Blairism endeavours to replicate the former gentry hegemony. In his Preface Smith quotes Peter Mandelson (of all people) as asking whether the 'era of representative democracy . . . is coming to a close'. The Task Force Report showed there to be no fewer than 295 such 'TFs', involving about 2500 'invitations to the party' (a phrase routinely used in their business). Smith continues: 'The Task Force Revolution may be another nail in the coffin of representative democracy [and] . . . other recent trends, such as the decline in the status of Parliament and a largely appointed Second Chamber, support the Mandelson view. We must therefore be on our guard lest the wider principles of election and accountability are diminished or jettisoned.' The reader will note the striking coincidence of numbers here: *2500* – the precise figure cited by Ellis Wasson in *Born to Rule*!

and devices for at least partial proportional representation. In the United Kingdom this is not so. As we saw, the result has been the odd bicephalic 'dictatorship' of 2000, founded upon stubborn resistance to any pro-founder alteration of course.

This implies something beyond 'autonomy'. One might say it favours the posture of an exaggerated or super-autonomy – something suggested indeed by the very rhetoric of Greatness and the traditions (or supposed traditions) of a sacred 'Sovereignty'. Each party must now not only become worthy of the narrative, but must ceaselessly *emphasise* its powers of narration. 'Redemptionism' means more than living up to the British past. It now entails outdoing that past, by novel and absolutely startling means. No empire can be recreated; but the imperium of Coolness, deft centrality and astute leadership can be presented as its natural son and heir.

In the 2001 election, against the backdrop of a blazing countryside and failing rail services, it had proved quite hard to maintain the Coolness crusade. However, the basic theme resurfaced in another way: 'Europe'. Since there was so little to hold an election about (other than upholding the dictatorship), various other electoral campaigns in effect took the place of Westminster's Official Campaign. In Northern Ireland the election was about the implementation (or not) of the Belfast Agreement of 1998. In Wales it was about advancing the National Assembly towards legislative power. In Scotland it was about the 'Barnett Formula' – that is, tax-raising powers for the new Scottish government, looking ahead to the next parliamentary elections for Holyrood, due in 2003.

But in England, it slipped sideways into a prolonged wrangle about how, when and if the UK should accept the European currency system. Nothing new was said about Europe. Excruciating platitudes failed to find their marks, and vanished as usual into oblivion. No 'decisions' interfered with the customary bowing and scraping about 'the National Interest' and Chancellor Brown's Five Commandments. Nothing whatever of significance happened until too late, with the Irish referendum vote against the Treaty of Nice (by coincidence this was also held on June 7th).

And yet, William Hague's election campaign, and indeed his entire party, tore itself to demented shreds around this 'nothing'. While Blair and Brown were demonstrating their easy command of vacuity, the Tories disappeared round the bend gibbering about Sovereignty, saving the pound, and keeping a European super-state at bay. In effect, New Labour was showing how well it wields Super-autonomous Sovereignty, while Conservatism was sinking into Europhobia – as its only hope of being able to continue wielding such power in the same way, when 'its turn' comes round at last. What the 'end of Britain' meant in this weird blue movie was more like the end of the post-1979 cycle – that is, of elective hyper-power, *real* authority based on grotesquely inflated 'majorities', with associated world-stage rights and 'freedom of action'. All we hold dear, in fact.[28]

Yet in the circumstances, there seemed no other way of living up to British exceptionalism. Providence could not be denied. To this deeply British mentality, the end of Empire has always felt like dawning

---

28 The link between 'The Pound' and 'All we hold dear' is quite an interesting one, although it has really nothing to do with the Euro currency as such. What people were furious about over this period was *identity*. But identity is much more intimately related to coinage and currency than is often realised. This is (obviously) likely to be particularly significant in a state so dependent upon exchange-values and foreign trading. Where (as in Britain) other concrete icons of identity are somewhat elusive, it is natural for people to identify unusually strongly – even pathologically strongly – with banknotes and the Queen's Head on coins. So *that* is what they want to abolish! To tread these underfoot is to walk upon the nation's soul and dreams. And to walk upon them most noticeably in London and the South-East, the traditional Tory heartland. A most important insight into this level of Britannic national identity has been provided by Kevin Barry, in his essay 'Paper Money and English Romanticism', in the *Times Literary Supplement*, 21 February 1997.

insignificance, not normality. It was instinctively felt as a slippage away from a divinely-designated greatness. All administrations since then have been compelled to be (or pretend to be) 'National' in the old, reverberant sense – all the more so, as the actual reverberations diminish, and an ordinary sort of sobriety begins to creep in. Since 'Britishness' was an external orientation rather than an ethnic root, there appeared no alternative to either prolonging or restoring the deep grammar of that former state and economy: an inheritor of the Burkean realm, as it were, only 'modernised'. Which invariably meant, modernised just as much as was good for it – with the City and the élite of a new generation in charge. Empirically *necessary* changes are naturally ever welcome, but only as long as they remain unaffected by the abstract foreign virus, constitutional stuff-and-nonsense.

Now shorn of overseas territories, the outreach of a revived commercial imperium of course sought the maximum in prestige and post-colonial standing. Being placed 'in the sun' and salient on the world stage does remain quite important to capital of this kind. It was not eclipsed by the loss of India, and certainly not by the crocodile tears of the Hong Kong withdrawal in 1998. The fundamental rôle of the United Kingdom state and its ideology, Britishness, is to hold eclipse in that sense at bay. A measure of democracy has come to be required for that task – but only the clinical minimum dosage recently praised by Professor Eric Hobsbawm, in an essay just before the election.[29]

---

29 'Democracy can be bad for you', in the *New Statesman*, 5 March 2001. 'Sidestepping the process of representative government' has become the British norm, groans Hobsbawm, '. . . increasing the citizens' distrust of government and lowering the public opinion of politicians.' But later he exaggerates, by extending the darkling plain of British anti-democracy to embrace the whole planet. Over increasing parts of planet Earth, democracy can be quite good for you, though only by implementation of simple democratic reforms which Britain's representative government has traditionally avoided.

Even in stumbling retreat, such a strong institutional complex is fated to reproduce itself. A state-nation like 'Great Britain' is likely to do so more determinedly than a nation-state, simply because there is in the end so little that is natural about it. For such a long-term by-product of conquest and class artifice, there can be little comfort in the last ditch. Combat alone will keep it 'surviving' there. While military effort may still have a rôle in this (as in the Falklands War, Blair's ventures in Kosovo and Sierra Leone, and the post-11 September reaction) it is *political* exertion that now counts most. This implies ideological régime-maintenance, beneath a representative façade. However, maintaining the façade has entailed installing a much-altered system beneath it, in the same way as a Georgian frontage may now hide offices or showrooms.

From the seventies down to the present, no incomer to Downing Street has escaped these pressures of Redemption – escaped the need (that is) to be far more than a mere administration, or a new package of policies. Both in 1979 and 1997 a more self-conscious sense of Providence materialised alongside the badges of Office.[30] It must not be forgotten that from

---

30 One notable feature of the forced retreat towards Englishness has been a re-surfacing of Providence – i.e. God, or Divine Will. The theme accords well enough with Blair's own Christian spiritualism. But the puzzle it poses is very tricky. Did God have 'England' or 'Britain' in mind all along? Historian Jonathan Clark points out that 'group identity in these islands is much older than its critics suppose . . . [and] predated the nineteenth century ideas about race and language that generated "nationalism". English identity even predated the Reformation, and . . . its keynote is Providential deliverance, a note heard repeatedly in our history'. When Professor Clark gets down to what the keynote *says*, however, disappointment awaits. As in all recent excursions of this kind, the writing on history's wall is banal platitudes: '. . . individuals, loyalty, public service, institutions, the rule of law . . .' (*Times*, 22 August 2000). *England*'s group identity has vanished once more, presumably into the care of Providence.

the forties up to 1979 both main British political movements had taken their turns at redressment in much humbler terms: lower-level or policy-package terms, almost always economic in reference. The complacency of those days was so great and so undisturbed, that politicians still felt policy-shifts alone might 'turn round the ship'. As long as the core-apparatus of grandeur remained unchallenged, it was tempting to believe that 'touches to the helm' might suffice, alternately from Left and Right. However, both the parties had tried this and failed miserably, time and time again. Only in the later 1970s did things get bad enough to put an end to such delusions, and force a more serious change of tempo and style.

This was why much more drastic therapy began to seem indispensable – why salvaging Greatness now demanded a 'régime', a Revolution, or a 'Project'. Implementing the right policies now involved making parallel changes to the system – either to society or to the state framework. Since forced-march Redemption was the motor of the endangered realm, there could be no escape: everybody had to be drummed into such pantomines – Thatcher's neo-liberal Enterprise Culture after 1979, and then Tony Blair's Third Way Project after 1997. We do not yet know what a new Conservative leader will follow on with in 2005 or 2006. At the time of writing Conservatism failed to mount a 'Great-again' recipe. In the leadership strife following their 2001 defeat, it sidelined the only figure who looked likely to rise to the occasion, Michael Portillo. However, 'transformism' now has to work both ways within the dual dictatorship of Britain. The Right did lead the way into full-blown Redemptionism, then found its formula purloined; but it is not unreasonable to think that it may yet re-enter this warped dialectic – or even become its culmination (or its nadir).

How misleading the metaphor of 'decline' has proved in the United Kingdom! The term conveys a sense of graduated loss or slippage, with a half-implication of indeterminate duration. That there has been British 'decline' in that sense, no party, leader or serious historian would deny. However, the concept carries within itself an enticing but potentially deadly counter-meaning: *revival* – the salvation, or even the renaissance, of whatever remains. After the disasters of Heath and Callaghan between 1970 and 1979, it is just this revivalist mentality that rose to the forefront – a 'make or break' ambition under which leadership was forced towards daily emphasis upon advances, 'radical'-seeming hopscotch, and transformations of the soul. As the *Economist* notes, Blair is indeed no 'declinist': he believes that Britain can lead, and is most herself when leading.

In other words, it is bright-eyed schemes of regeneration which have dominated the actual 'decline' (one can now say 'collapse') of the UK's *'ancien régime'*. No earlier prophecies of imperial slide or decay took this into account. In the strange fall into oblivion that really occurred, 'Radicalism' came to be appropriated as the *leitmotiv* of the foundering process itself.[31] From 1979 onwards, different leaders have of course wielded contrasting policy recipes and ideal vistas, of Left and Right, Europe or USA-oriented. But all have been ostensibly 'radical', in the sense of would-be thorough and decisive, settling matters for good. This striving for reinstatement has consistently been counterfeited as drama-filled release, a leap forward: the advent of Astraea, 'the corn-bearing Virgin whose return to earth signifies the end of the cycle of decline through the ages of brass, iron and lead, and the coming again of the

---

31 The mutations in 'radicalism' over the past decade call for a book in themselves. The 2001 election of course brought a farther shift, registered by Anthony Howard in his *Times* column of 12 June 2001. Even after four years, he sourly observes, 'Blair's party has not yet tumbled to the fact that when he uses the word "radical" he really means "right-wing" – and it is in for a nasty shock'.

golden years'.[32] Hysterical countermanding by the reigning will has sought to screen the melancholia of retreat.

Everything has had to be transformed and re-transformed, not (in Count Lampedusa's famous phrase) to let them 'go on as before', but so that they can be immensely, improbably better. The psychology of bankruptcy is very close to that of the conman, or Thomas Mann's hypnotist: a projection of bedazzled betterment and rejuvenation, of traditions undergoing stylish cure by 'modernisation', with élan and up-to-the minute techniques. Never has prestidigitation been so powerful. The public's attention has to be distracted from the collapse of the stage itself, by the futurological fireworks being enacted upon it.

Yet could it be otherwise? Since the tradition being served is in essence so extraordinary ('Providence', the proverbial thousand years, Mother of all Parliaments, etc.) its Salvation can be no less spectacular. It belongs upon the plane of wars, historic initiatives and exemplary vanguardism. It means placing oneself at the forefront (or 'at the heart') of whatever seems to matter most for the moment. Like Thatcher before him, Blair in turn announced no less than a *revolution* in 1997. The old axis of commercial–financial empire was once quietly sustained by a symbiotic social caste. In the latter's absence, it can only be supported by ever-noisier swashbuckling like President Bush's 'Star Wars', or dazzling sorties on to any stage where Leadership seems for a time to be lacking.

And indeed this is still why reluctant electors were so abruptly hustled

---

32 I owe this insight to Professor Bruce Lenman, the great historian of Jacobitism. See the chapter 'Thatcherite epilogue: *Reductio ad absurdum* or *Plus ça change . . . ?'* in his *The Eclipse of Parliament: Appearance and Reality in British Politics since 1914* (Arnold 1992), p. 261. Professor Lenman traces the antecedents of end-game Britishness back to a longer-running degeneration of the eighteenth century Constitution, from World War I onwards.

into polling stations in 2001. To outsiders, it may well have looked as if a late-seventeenth-century cadaver was tottering into a family mausoleum (itself visibly disintegrating). But surviving members of the family are conditioned to perceive things very differently. They find themselves filing on regardless, like Cavaliere Cipolla's seaside public of eighty years ago, deluded (or maybe now only half-deluded) by the promise of a brilliant afterlife.

The alternative is reform, but in the sense of constitutional change rather than of smart plumbing plus cultural fireworks. The 2001 election successfully kept reform out of the picture. Much credit was claimed for Devolution, and for the Ulster Peace process, but not as way-stations or precedents, leading onwards to more substantial transformation. These were exemplifications of an Immaculate Essence, rather than pointers towards a new faith. The bicephalic tyranny of Greatness was successfully projected onwards into still another century – 'exaltation of the autonomous agent unhindered by outside control', for all time to come (or at least, until the rail-track finally gives way). The persistence of Tidrick's 'primitive conception of the nature of authority' was granted a farther lease of life – and we can be sure New Labour will defend this to its own death. In it British Socialism finally gave up its soul to Satan, British nationalism; and it is unlikely to escape paying the price.

4   THE GLOW FROM THE PAST

We started the second half of 20th century with a hopelessly false self-image, especially – and understandably – after our Finest Hour. Other countries such as Germany and Japan have tried to bury their ghosts . . . We have fought not to do so.

Christopher Patten, British Council Independent Lecture, summarised in the *Independent*, 29 June 2001

To understand the unshakability of Chris Patten's 'remarkable achievement' and Westminster's accompanying grandeur-obsession, it may also be important to recall how it had been underscored by relatively recent events. Most people think back instinctively to Mrs Thatcher's South Atlantic war triumph of the 1980s. But in his study *Iron Britannia* (1982) Anthony Barnett showed how the reflexes of that moment went back in turn to what he labelled 'Churchillism', a complex inherited from World War II which united the conviction of world centrality with the impossibility of defeat and humiliation.[33] Not only the Falklands victory but post-World War II Britain has been sustained by the long-range repercussions of what happened on a single, hot evening in May 1940.

That was the instant when the Victorian apparatus of rule – already under serious strain, its collapse quite widely predicted – was redeemed by Winston Churchill. The study I mentioned before, John Lukacs's *Five Days in London, May 1940* (2000), has recently re-examined the astonishing hourly detail of how this happened, between the 23rd and the 28th of May, 1940. On that last day Churchill finally over-rode the temporising and cautious spirits in his Cabinet and decided that Britain would fight on 'no matter what happened' at Dunkirk or anywhere else. He left the House of Commons, went to Admiralty House and sent a telegram to the French Premier Paul Reynaud refusing Mussolini's offer to 'intercede' with the Germans. Later he summarised the event in *Their Finest Hour* (1949): 'It fell to me . . . to

---

33 'From the aristocrats of finance-capital to the auto-didacts of the trade unions, the war created a social and political amalgam which was not a fusion – each component retained its individuality – but which nonetheless transformed them all internally, inducing in each its own variety of Churchillism and making each feel essential for the whole. Today, Churchillism has degenerated into a chronic deformation, the sad history of contemporary Britain . . .'. This was written in 1982, *nineteen years ago.* Anthony Barnett, *Iron Britannia*, (Allison 1982).

express the sentiments [of the people] on suitable occasions. This I was able to do, because they were mine also. There was a white glow, overpowering, sublime, which ran through our island from end to end.' The reckless adventurer had saved his class, as no prudent calculator or economist could ever have done. He knew within himself that if the compromises urged by the faint-hearts were made, British greatness would indeed be at an end: one adroit compromise or half-surrender would lead to another, in a spiral of apparent reasonableness with prostration at its end. The result would be betrayal rather than honourable defeat. The latter comported frightful risks; but from the former, he understood that no recovery would ever be possible. A popular mood resonated with this inner certainty, and enabled the overpowering sentiment he described.

Thus, against the commercial grain of its own nature, the British élite was granted a unique, high-temperature reprieve which restored its popular authority, and its associated ideogram of national meaning. Empires have always tended to inflate ethnocentricity into a religion. But in this case the longer *durée* of *Pax Britannica* had discovered *in extremis* an extraordinary window of what was to become long-term (and then terminal) justification. In effect, the United Kingdom (as Lukacs argues) actually *was* for a very short time the hinge of world history. It could never have defeated the Third Reich, but it did make sure that the war was not lost *then*, in ways which might in turn have altered the whole later pattern of conflict. Transient as that role was, it proved enough to hard-wire all the existing stigmata of Providence and British self-importance, and bestow upon them sixty years of farther life.

Jim Bulpitt refers to the victory of 'the Churchill gang' in 1940; the term is justified – but it must be acknowledged that this group was in essence the same extended cousinhood as that evoked in Ingham's conclusion, cited above. Kathryn Tidrick underlines its nature in the Epilogue to *Empire and the English Character*. Although it had to be dragged into final decision by charismatic guidance, it was nothing like the Iron Heel of left-wing legend. This élite came from 'mechanisms which were developed to ensure that the imperial demand for leadership met with an unfailing supply (from) a governing class through which the leadership ethos was thoroughly diffused. In a land where the public school system produced *Führers* on the wholesale principle, there was no prospect of any one of them arriving at supreme power.'[34] Early-modern gangland (in that sense) was far stronger than fascism; in pastiche-form it still endures in today's 'Blairism', where it continues to serve Ingham's 'deeply entrenched forces of tradition' in the City and elsewhere.

In the time beyond, during the Cold War – when so much would be fossilised or held over by the stalemate of the victors – Churchill's fading 'white glow' was to remain the core of the British ruling instinct. Its nobility was to infuse the decrepit paraphernalia of the old outward-looking State, and award it two farther generations of existence. If Blair feels twilight advancing, what this means is that the 1940 drug must really be wearing off. Yet even now an intimate Ukanian reflex is not ready for withdrawal symptoms. All it can do is call for stronger doses of methadone. At bottom the Redemption-régimes of late-twentieth-century Britain have crumbled into parasites of their own past. Their new starts and clarion-calls are also so many crusades to rekindle the fading light, and project it forward into another century of exceptionalism.

The story of the Greenwich Millennium Dome encapsulated all these motifs into the later 1990s. When New Labour won office in 1997 one of its most urgent choices was whether or not to proceed with the project. Recollections of the success of Attlee's Festival of Britain in 1951 had to compete with dread of possible failure, and a cost-conscious opposition rendered more militant by the climate of Thatcherite economics. At a

---

34 Tidrick, *Empire and the English Character*, pp. 279–80.

critical moment the *Times* journalist (and former Editor) Simon Jenkins
wrote Blair a personal letter containing the following comments:

> I understand you are eager to know what will make your children want
> to go to Greenwich. Let me tell you. Greenwich will be the world's one
> big Millenium celebration . . . German, French, Italian and American
> planners all concede Britain's leadership here. Every child, including
> many from abroad, will want 'to see Greenwich in 2000' and tell it to
> their grandchildren. Such events are milestones in a nation's history . . .
> I promise you, Greenwich is a future that will work. It will be Britain's
> proudest creation and proudest boast in the Year 2000 . . . (quoted in
> Adam Nicolson, *Regeneration: The Story of the Dome* (1999), p. 143)

The mission behind the Dome was the reincarnation and transmission of
the white glow. At that time, the resurrectionists thought themselves capable of anything. Under Peter Mandelson's guidance, the project then went
ahead, with the disaster-laden conclusion known to everyone (including
quite a few from abroad). One of the minor astonishments of the 2001
election was the low profile the failure had in the months leading up to the
election of 2001. Such a dismal catastrophe should itself have brought any
government down, or at least severely affected its electoral support. That it
did not, illustrates the power of New Labour's publicity machine. What the
new gang lacks in real cousinhood it can make up for to some extent with
chutzpah and non-stop rhetoric.

There was between 1997 and 2001 a residual lack of confidence in New
Labourism, derived from its years in the political desert as well as from
echoes of the former upper-class hegemony. They behaved as if unable
quite to credit the transformation that had taken place, half-thinking the
'natural rulers' might yet reassert themselves. After 2001, this will surely
diminish. As Anne McElvoy has put it, 'We're all Blairites now':

Nowadays, the 'centre-left' is an almost meaningless phrase. New Labour's centre is so big that it has swallowed up most of the range of political opinion. Even those intending to use their vote tactically to diminish Labour's majority or stamp on the prostrate Tory body, are effectively confirming the grip of the new status quo. To that extent, we are all Blairites now. In the process, it has become the party of the opportunists, the hangers-on, the timeservers and the brazenly self-interested. It has developed the flaws of the powerful and successful. It finds it difficult to impose restrictions or moral stringency on itself. (*Independent*, 6 June , 2001)

The week following the election result, government Ministers announced a substantial pay rise for themselves. Where formerly they might have delayed the news, and coughed modestly about it being overdue and well-earned, mounting confidence enabled the powerful and successful simply to state the facts. The latter impacted upon a citizenry which a few days previously had manifested the deepest cynicism about politicians. But this was no longer important. Things were settling down.

In truth, all the successive stage-act novelties leading to this *dénouement* have achieved is postponement of what the British countries most needed from 1945 onwards. Genuine radicalism lay not in British Socialism but in *democratic* overhaul, and advance towards a contemporary constitution. The 2001 vote was preceded by a pathetic appeal in the letter page of the *Times* from Lord Jenkins and others, urging the public not to forget electoral reform altogether:

In 1998, as members of the Independent Commission on the Voting System, we recommended changing Britain's primitive first-past-the-post system . . . [and] . . . as the present election progresses, the disadvantages of the system are suddenly more manifest. In particular, there is a real prospect that turnout will plunge, as many voters see that

their votes will not count. We look to the Government to hold a referendum on our proposals as early as possible in the next Parliament.
(*Times*, 3 June 2001)

Both the proposals and the prophecy were justified. However, it is less
the Government than the larger system which should be blamed. What
terminal Britishness really echoes (and now falls back on with added
relish) is itself something 'primitive': Kathryn Tidrick's 'governing
ethos' with its 'exaltation of the autonomous agent unhindered by outside
control, its primitive conception of the nature of authority'. The death
throes seem to have made this worse. Blair felt forced into setting up
Jenkins's Independent Commission by lingering uncertainty; but as the
inferiority complex evaporated, so did his interest in proportional representation.

Such reforms would represent a fairly drastic tack away from the whole
commercial–imperial legacy – a distinct turning towards nation-state
normality, modest and yet incompatible with Westminsterism. There was
no chance that a Conservative administration would embark on this mun-
dane course. But New Labourism has become equally tied to British
destiny – on occasion even more so, as if to allay whatever suspicions of
'unsoundness' may still attach to it. The usual left-wing critique of
Labourite moderation has been its wish to appease *capitalism*; but this
appears secondary to its British nationalism. Up to the time of James
Callaghan, British Socialism was always 'British' first, and Socialist a long
way second. In fact it believed socialism to be mostly quite unrelated to
constitutional matters – a matter of 'policy' and administration, rather
than of democracy.

The raggle-taggle successors to 'National Government' which have
imposed themselves since 1979 are a system of alternating caretakers for
Britishness and this version of post-imperial identity. They seem to be

serving the City and 'Roseland' well enough.[35] 2001 signalled at once the further congealment of this system, and – in the anti-political sullenness or resentment of the voters – some incipient reaction against it. Post-'79 Redemptionism was indeed a 'break', in the sense of a rejection of the former decay-consensus, what commentators once labelled as 'Butskellism'. But instead of constitutional reform, the rupture has taken the form of a progressive coarsening and brutalisation of the old apparatus itself. Rather than being replaced, Westminsterism has been transformed into the present tightening straitjacket of alternating dictatorships.

The 2001 election underlined one very significant form of response to the shrinking system: abstention. On the eve of the contest the *Guardian*'s Assistant Editor David McKie published a warning article about what he called 'the non-voting party'. In 1997, he pointed out, non-voters had come second to Blair's New Labour, ending just over 2 per cent behind the victors: 28.6 per cent as against 30.9 per cent (the Conservatives having won only 21.9 per cent). He concluded that '[a]s the 2001 election approaches, it looks as though the Non-Voting Party might be set for its best result ever.'[36] Never was a prophecy so well rewarded. On June 7th the 'NVP' won a sensational 15 per cent victory over Blair's 'winning party'. Electoral participation slumped from 1997's 72 per cent down to 59 per cent – the lowest total since David Lloyd-George's notorious 'Khaki Election' in 1918. Since at that time the UK franchise was incompletely modernised, was in fact simply the lowest turnout in the UK *democratic* era (or what passes for it).

---

35 'Rest-of-the-South-East' land or 'Roseland' took over from former ideas like the metropolitan 'golden circle' in the 1990s. It means in fact the 'city-state' – or perhaps more precisely, the '*City*-state' country, in relation to which other parts of Great Britain have become so many 'hinterlands'.

36 *The Guardian Companion to the 2001 General Election*, edited by Julian Glover (Atlantic Books 2001) pp. 122–4.

Eve-of-poll predictions had confined themselves to imagining a 'disastrous' percentage decline to the lower sixties.

As the Editor of the *Times Literary Supplement* (15 June) later put it: 'The landslide victory of the Apathetic Tendency took most commentators by surprise, although they pretended to have foreseen it coming . . . Yet politicians and commentators seem somewhat reluctant to address this question.' They had no plausible explanation to hand. But neither has Editor Ferdinant Mount, himself the author of a comparatively recent and often penetrating account of the British Constitution.[37] On this occasion he opts for the Contentment thesis: voters are mainly fairly pleased with their lives, and consequently less concerned with politics. This 'de-intensifying of British politics' has been caused by familiar enough things: 'no inflation or unemployment to speak of, rising living standards, no civil strife, no foreign wars, and general agreement between parties on the fundamentals of economic and social management'. 'Is this bad?' he asks rhetorically – or, '[m]ay

---

37 *Recovering the Constitution* (Charter 88 1992). It is worth stressing that *ten years ago* Mount could complain of the disgraceful pantomine which the House of Commons had come to represent:

> It is here in the House of Commons that one experiences the rustiness of our system at its most painful and embarrassing. It is not simply the habitual emptiness of the Chamber, now crowded only for the hollow mummery of Prime Minister's question time, it is the emptiness of the speeches; the listless drone of the Minister reading out his brief, the unconvincing chuckles of the doughnut ring around him, the unconvincing jeers of the Opposition, the members who have been persuaded to stay on for the debate on the promise of unspecified favours from the Whips. True, much of all this would be familiar to observers of the House of Commons in its supposed heyday; in fact, I have often thought that the most shocking sight to the novice – the backbenchers who have been pressed to serve on committees, and who appear to spend most of their time on answering their letters – needs only a few stove-pipe hats and brocade waistcoats to recall the Parliaments of the Regency.

abstaining be not merely the refuge of the catatonic and the disenchanted, but a sleepy assent to a different kind of politics?'

But no one noticed much sleepy assent during the fuel crises of 2000, or in Oldham, or in Northern Ireland, or in Scotland and Wales, where what were really quite different election campaigns had been fought, and turnout was now perceived as 'for Westminster'. This implied that in these places quite non-apathetic voters now felt they could either take it or leave it. Even in England, vast numbers certainly experienced no 'never-had-it-so-good' feelings about either Blair or the unconvincing alternatives on offer. However much they resented or feared the *status quo*, there was nothing most of them could 'do' about it; except of course, to stay at home, cursing 'the lot of them'. In the week before the vote a number of public voices had also taken up the 'cause' of abstention, and declared their non-voting intentions. This is surely not 'de-intensification' so much as a straightforward alienation of the electorate, provoked by an increasingly deformed and spurious mode of government.

'But it's the same everywhere!' became the sheepish bleat of all Blairite apologists in the wake of the 2001 vote. Cut-price universalism of this sort is a standard last refuge for scoundrels hoist upon their own petard. Since the United Kingdom is the pivot of political Creation, all that afflicts it has to be universal. No débâcle can ever be due to 'Britain' floundering in its own self-made last ditch. Nor could voter apathy conceivably be Westminster's fault for indulging in years of determined depoliticisation and dumb-down populism, or for postponing more serious democratic reform. No: general collapse of civilised standards is the obvious explanation. 'Western' populations must all be 'assenting sleepily to this different kind of politics'. If this is so, then it is but right that the UK should lead the way. A resolute move towards mass inertia is preferable to trailing in the rearguard, among old-fashioned democrats. Britishness means being at the heart of things, even of universal cynicism.

Instead of blessed ordinariness, therefore, from 1979 onwards HM's subjects have been consoled with the iron sacraments of neo-liberalism, Margaret Thatcher, the Falklands War, fake Americanisation, and then more recently New Labour's successor to British Socialism, the Third Way – and a subsequent 'resignation' of half the electorate. All this and the Dome as well. But have not all these been so many ways of clinging to the Churchillian fantasms of centrality and exceptionalism: that is, the salvation and renewal of an 'identity' worn too close to the skin to be discardable? The English have been made to feel that this skin, 'Britishness', is like their Monarchy: what makes them special. Without these indispensable uniforms, they would be worse than naked. They would be 'little English', a stark ethnicity bereft of all past vectors of significance and direction.

5   THE THREAT OF ORDINARINESS

It has never been John Bull's way to bother about forms, provided the facts are to his liking. He has no scruple in making the best of both worlds, and keeping the Empire as he keeps the Crown, stripped of all but the shadow of its original meaning, but all the more important as a symbol and bond of unity, the stimulant of a far nobler than imperial pride . . .

Esmé Wingfield-Stratford, *Foundations
of British Patriotism* (1940), p. 409

A most interesting analysis of the late-British political machinery was made recently by Oxford University political scientist Ross McKibbin, and deserves quoting at length:

The aim of the Blair government is to depoliticize political action. That
however comes not from a coherent theory of democracy but from the
legacy of its predecessor, whose aim was also depoliticization: under the
Conservatives the average voter was conceived as a customer, a client, a
consumer, an investor – anything but a politically active citizen.
Depoliticization . . . was to be achieved by a central state whose powers
were not only undiminished but in many ways increased. In this respect
too, New Labour is very much the child of Old Labour, many of whose
deepest attachments were to the British state and its constitutional apparatus. That two such self-consciously innovative governments as
Thatcher's and Blair's cannot really break with the dominant traditions
of British government lends support to Tocqueville's view, that any society, however revolutionary its rhetoric or behaviour, however good its
democratic intentions, finds it exceptionally difficult to depart from the
political and constitutional structure it inherits . . . ('Treading Water',
New Left Review, new series, No. 4, July–August 2000)

But at the same time as the 'deepest attachments' were being put on this
diet of heedless populism, the most damnable developments were proceeding abroad. The tidal wave of neo-liberalism and the end of State
Socialism were certainly quite favourable to a conservation of Britishness
in the short term. However, they did bring with them a disconcerting new
phenomenon. In the post-Cold War world, small and desperately ordinary
nations were flourishing as never before.

Scandinavia was bad enough. This year, Sweden, Norway and Finland
have become the 'dominant information economies' of the world, leaving
the USA in fourth position. 'Somehow the staid Swedes – strangers to
hire-and-fire, averse to risk and famously useless as bullshitters – have
come to lead the business revolution', remarked *Industry Standard Europe*
in the Spring of 2001. As if that were not humiliation enough, it began to
look as if a country no metropolitan big-hitter had ever taken seriously at

all may be on the point of joining the Baltic vanguard: *Ireland*, for God's sake.

How 'ordinary' can you get? Ireland was not even in the house. It was a lean-to hen-coop somewhere in the farmyard. In fact it was the sub-ordinary reverse of everything Britannic greatness had stood for – small, rural, faith-obsessed, 'ethnic', quaint and devoted to 'irrational' violence. In 1940 one of the great trombones of British nationalism, Esmé Wingfield-Stratford, dismissed Ireland's 1922 *de facto* separation in these terms:

> Britain's loss, such as it was, resembled that of a malignant tumour . . . An Irelandless Britain was in every way a healthier and stronger Britain. And there was at least the chance – and to those with faith in British principles more than the chance – that when the inflamed bitterness of ages had had time to heal, a free Ireland might turn out to be an asset, at long last, instead of a liability to British civilization.

By the close of the twentieth century this no-hoper had become the world's leading exporter of computer software. IBM is planning to make Dublin the centre for its entire European and Middle Eastern operation in the century to come. By February 2002 it would be singled out by *Foreign Policy* magazine's 'Globalisation Index' as 'the most globalised nation on earth'.[38] The volcanic mode of economic development that so consistently eluded Harold Wilson, Mrs Thatcher and the other Elders of Britishness, has come to be taken for granted in the Kingdom's former backyard. And – as if to rub the point in – it has done so largely without the avalanche of bullshit which since 1979 has weighed so heavily upon all of London's Redemption strategies.

This is simply intolerable: the world is being stood on its head. It is

---

38 *Foreign Policy*, Jan.–Feb. 2002, pp. 38–51, 'The A.T.Kearney/*Foreign Policy* Globalisation Index, a Ranking of Economic and Political Integration in 62 Countries'.

difficult enough to depart from Tocqueville's 'inherited political and constitutional structure', let alone face a conversion owing *nothing* to British Civilisation. Something is amiss with the Firmament. If nobody can now turn into somebody, this means that somebody could turn into nobody. So London may soon be no more important than Singapore, and Paris could sink to the level of Helsinki? Ukania's outreach mode of governance was always intended to dispel the very thought of such a Fall. In the post-Cold War universe, the magic of time itself seems to be faltering: 'this way madness lies' – as indeed it does, above all (I shall go on to argue) for the English.

Everything else follows from Tocqueville's point. The populism McKibbin describes expresses the régime's absolute need to 'mould' opinion its own way – and so avoid that mutinous tendency which unaccountably spread under Mrs Thatcher (and finally destroyed her). Yet this tendency grows year on year, like some gathering earthquake mysteriously aggravated by 'globalisation' itself. Up at Westminster its effects continue to be in the main refracted through an optic of mildewed grandeur. The latter permits only the perception that *even greater* authority is now required. Still longer ranges of time will be needed to counteract the toxin, even larger majorities are called for, more think-tanks have to be set up – or at least Task Forces, or Commissions. Ideological regimentation needs ever cooler and more comely forms, like the retreaded House of Lords.

But the basic apparatus is *not* for replacing: thoughtful modification on a basis of genuflection remains the Kingdom's chosen mode of advance. Knee-pads are still better than skates. In Kathryn Tidrick's phrase, the thing to look for is 'loving awe from the governed', the lubricant which has always kept the antique going (with occasional jabs of 'There is No Alternative!'). Loving awe exacts three sideways shuffles for every inch forward. This is why no truly British government now feels safe without these colossal majorities, and without making subjects feel it will

stay in office 'for ever' (that is, for an unforeseeable, or possibly generational, period of time). Greatness demands Sovereignty, with that capital
'S'. Efficacious Authority in return demands the appearance of omnipotence – a 'consensus' summoned up from above, by overwhelming
cunning and cultural glamour, and somehow fated to triumph against all
odds. Every few years voters must be summoned to show their pre-packed
'consent'.

At this point it is useful to go back to the political schemas cited earlier
from Dennis Kavanagh and Jim Bulpitt: lethal electoralism, adversarialism,
surrogate élitism, the absence of pluralism, an unwritten Constitution and
a 'Court politics' which entailed that 'only national office is worth gaining:
losing office – elections – means the political wilderness'. These were diag-
noses influenced by Thatcher's government of the 1980s, but they were also
looking backwards rather than forwards. In effect, they were perceiving a
traditional state-order in the earlier stages of derangement. Decline had
begun to mutate into something worse, but it was not yet clear what the
farther shore would be like. Now we are stranded on it, and can hardly help
knowing better. 'The legacy of Blair's predecessor' (as McKibbin puts it)
has developed into a perfect specimen of *trasformismo* – phoney rupture
into a successor '-ism' which bears forward elements from both Right and
Left. In other words, it is *national*: a successor state-nation paradigm, not
limited to one or other Party inheritance or policy-set. The '-ism' that
really counts is the assumed mantle and aureole of the United Kingdom
state: British nationalism.

'Overwhelming' remains the name of this British game. It was superbly
demonstrated in the earlier stages of the foot-and-mouth crisis. When the
disease started to spread seriously, Westminster (embodied by the unfor-
tunate Nicholas Brown, Minister for Agriculture) simply issued a
Churchillian edict: '*Stay out of the Countryside!*' Three weeks later the
tourism industry was beginning to collapse, and hoteliers were joining

the ranks of the despairing and suicidal farmers. A second Biblical injunction then resounded from the same source: '*Get back into the Countryside! Holiday at Home!*' It had been an offence to holiday at home; now it was a sin to holiday abroad. At the same moment, Mr Blair took over the struggle in person. He paid a prodigiously publicised and overall-clad Churchillian visit to the slaughter-fields of Cumbria, before ordering an all-out Army assault upon the virus. His subjects were told to fight on, in the stockyards, in the fields, upon the funeral pyres, thus according New Labour sufficient time for Greatness.

There was no evidence that any of these campaigns were necessary, or had much effect on the disease. There was no real substance to the 180° switch from one week to the next. Its point was to appear overwhelming. These were not so much commands as specimens of Ukanian 'commandism': floor shows intended to reassure the populace at a deeper psychic level, by the evocation of firm central power, ever resolute and 'in control'. In truth, foot-and-mouth was not overwhelmed, and nobody was in control of anything. Policy oscillated crazily from one improvisation to another: *Götterdammerung* burnings, vast burial pits, military manoeuvres and mass vaccination, punctuated by protests from embittered farmers and complaints from the UK's trade partners. The sole point of general agreement was that 'MAFF' (the Ministry of Agriculture, Food & Fisheries) had throughout shown itself to be a disgrace, deserving of abolition rather than the new style of 'radical reform'.

One week before the election, Channel 4 TV News conducted a provisional investigation of the episode, in which penitent officials and 'experts' confessed they might have got things 'a bit wrong', and suggested that only a Public Inquiry would ever sort it out. Mr Blair at onced riposted with the perfect régime proposal: yes, there must be a *proper* inquiry, carried out by the proper people. The instinctive calculation of proper authority had all along been that, bemused or not, a depoliticised folk would understand the firm smack of Authority. Proper inquiries can be relied on to endorse populism. Full Public Inquiries, on the other hand, draw in the rabble, malcontents, resignations, threats of prosecution, and a general demeaning of power. On the point of awarding itself a second 'landslide majority', New Labour was reluctant to risk any appearance of reasonable indecision.

It was also noticeable throughout the cloven-hoof epidemic how each futile step of New Labour's policy was vocally determined by one factor: *how it looks abroad*. 'What will they think?' in Washington, Moscow, Peking and elsewhere – this seems to have been the question that really tortured Downing Street, alongside the possibility of being less than overwhelming in their second term of office. There was naturally some comment on the disaster in adjoining countries like Ireland, the Netherlands and France, where the contagion showed signs of spreading. After the previous history of BSE and Creutzfeldt-Jakob's disease, this is not surprising. But elsewhere very few observers 'thought' anything at all, or even knew that the Ukanian countryside was in trouble. And if any rumour did reach them, it was merely as confirmation of a previously low estimate reached over a very long time.

In its terminal mode, Ukanian politics has become less a choice between two parties than a matter of 'going for' one or other elective autocracy – when the dictatorship in charge allows, invariably at a moment calculated to prolong its own rule in the direction of eternity. The *ancien régime* used to favour an alternation of parties as a way of maintaining stability, the most prized virtue of the old nineteenth-century state. But its deformed inheritor has transformed evolutionism into a periodical (and accidental) oscillation between Salvationist crusades. Every fifteen to twenty years there is a hiccup: '*Events*, dear boy, events!' But by then another team will (it is assumed) be on stand-by, rehearsed and poised for the burden of Pivot-power.

Within these new constraints, both defeat and victory have wholly altered their meaning. Nowadays, the government of Ukania is only worth having as the power to change . . . well, practically everything, on paper. But in practice very little *can* change, within the inherited parameters of state. The outreach economy is more completely in the saddle than ever before, it is kept there by its own Bank of England – not even by the mainly compliant Treasury Chancellors of yore – and London and 'Roseland' daily augment their hegemony over the rest of 'Britain'. Hence the real power has become one over souls – that is, whatever is required to keep the white-glow *Geist* in business, the standing and influence of the state. In the teeth of adversity, 'Britishness' must to herself be true, through Leadership-will, non-stop exhortation, and Sovereignly radical posturing upon the world stage. But the obverse of such victory is that 'defeat' no longer signifies simply a few years of oppositional retreat or rethinking: it has come to represent soul-death, abject humiliation, a wilderness of worthlessness, and decade-long struggles for revival.

Once ejected from the Salvation business – necessarily by some accident, or an uncontrollable surge out of 'the depths' – a UK political party no longer has any recognisable meaning or doctrine to defend. How can it? Left versus Right has disappeared. 'Greatness' is securely back in 'Britain' all right: but as an inescapable strait-jacket, from which exit gets less and less conceivable. Under such circumstances, the Party either *is* the State-nation – Greatness *redevivus* – or it is not. Suffering the latter fate no longer means merely being sidelined, it is more like being unmasked, discarded, dismissed into the howling wilderness. Many years are then needed to concoct some pseudo-meaning under which the banner of Greatness may again be seized.

In his *New Yorker* 'Letter from London', Joe Klein describes meeting the former Director of Blair's No. 10 Policy Unit, David Miliband, who told him: 'We have set all our sticks out on the ground . . . but we haven't figured out how to rub them together and make fire yet'.[39] This level of policy-formation appears appropriate to Tidrick's 'primitive conception of authority'. When an even smaller minority finally supports it, such power may have to give way to the other tribe. But only when the current witch-doctorate has been exposed, humiliated and vomited out of business. In the meantime, 'Opposition' must simply think-tank the time away as best it can – attending patiently in Limbo until a tidal wave of nausea builds up somewhere below the horizon. The 'Get the Rascals Out!' super-roller will come in all right, but its timing is quite unpredictable. Till then, the surfers must chill out on the beach and keep their boards dry.

Such was the fate of Labour after 1979, and then of the Tories after 1997. It does not seem to occur to the New Labourites that the pitiable system they so ardently embrace, must in time force them out upon the same wasteland of disgrace and ridicule. *Their* retinue of place-persons, busybody groups, quangos, advisers, think-tanks and opinion-moulders will then have to flee for shelter across the plain, to be replaced by another 2500 – somewhat younger and hungrier Sinners, even more Justified and less scrupulous than those who went before.

Redemption has turned out to have its own rules, in fact; and so does the inevitable Fall from Redemption. Euphoric bedazzlement *can* end only in savage disappointment, as a disappointed people comes to feel again the daily slippage from Grace, and the mounting stench of careerist sleaze. 'Apathy' is just a phase of the cycle, the one so much in evidence before the 2001 election. But the Governments of parody-Britain have learned how

---

39 *New Yorker*, 4 June 2001, p. 42. Mr Miliband's anguish was soon to be alleviated by the election itself. He was, in the current centralist *argot*, 'parachuted' into the ultra-safe Labour Party constituency of South Shields, Tyne and Wear, after the previous MP, David Clarke, had been persuaded to retire . . . to the House of Lords.

quickly this can turn into hatred and rejection. Ceaseless public relations may keep the latter at bay for long enough. Eventually, however, the magic will fail, leaving as the sole possibility a lurch over into whatever 'alternative' version of Redemption-lunacy is available.

Thus has a former élite indifference to ideas and abstract notions been replaced by the hectic vertigo and style-obsession of today. Stability has metamorphosed into lurching instability – periodic tidal-wave lurches from one 'vision' or project to the next in line. The phlegm of Edmund Burke's old Britain has dissolved into a ceaseless contest of exactly the sort of brainstorms he most detested, like Thatcher's Poll Tax and Blair's Millenium Dome. These produce in turn a cumulative popular cynicism, occasionally vented in riots or the 'fuel protests' of last year. This climate of menace in turn exacerbates both the populist mania of the rulers – a simulacrum of democracy – and their abject dependence upon tabloid press and dumbed-down TV.

The mentality of this precarious élite grows more susceptible both to personal relations in its court (including personality disorders) and to conspiratorial *coups d'état* like the one which evicted Thatcher in 1990.[40]

---

40 The 'courts' of Thatcher and Blair have been able to perform as simulacra of the former ruling class only by the formation of weird synthetic 'families' or quasi-kinship networks where personal relations and rivalries can assume fulcral significance. The most riveting account of how this has worked in Blairism is that given by a journalist formerly sympathetic to New Labour, Andrew Rawnsley, in *Servants of the People: the Inside Story of New Labour* (Hamish Hamilton 2000). An important source on the grander patronage 'network' controlled from Westminster is the *Fifth Report* of the House of Commons Public Administration Committee, *Mapping the Quango State*, Vol. 1, March 2001. The *Report* makes use of an earlier study by the Local Government Information Unit, 'The Advance of the Quango State', and quietly points out how '[t]hese developments are not bedded down in democratic arrangements' – hence there is an urgent need for more *English* democracy (p. xxxix).

The bizarre sub-plot of Peter Mandelson has illustrated this most famously in New Labour's first term, but there are many others: the unforgiving feuds of a synthetic 'extended family', without which neither Party nor Government can now carry on. Blairism is still some way from John Major's plight in the nineties: at the time of writing, no clique has yet been publicly dismissed as 'those bastards!'. But time is also likely to tell. In such perfect greenhouse conditions, another coup is probably already under way, after the effects of June 2001 wear off.

I know one must be careful with such verdicts. Criticisms of a successor or 'synthetic' élite is always liable to slide into an implied nostalgia for the original or 'natural' product – in this case the great-oak, landowning-and-mercantile class of Edmund Burke. Yet that would be grotesque. Surely it is natural for new societies to foster new power-groups, and indeed produce what theorists have described as a 'circulation of élites'? So what (it may be asked) is so wrong with being 'artificial', or with society inventing new forms of rule – is that not what democracies are supposed to do?

Of course it is: it is what *democracies* are meant to do. But parody-Britain is not a democracy. It is a diseased descendant of representative oligarchy, which has consistently refused to reform central power democratically. Instead it has settled for the lowest common denominator, a national populism of last resort. In June 2001 this resulted in a general election decisively won by the non-voters. Simple extrapolation would suggest there will soon be no point in voting at all, and governments could be changed by sessions of *Big Brother* where people are allowed to show which 'candidate' they hate most. 'The language of greatness' (in Bulpitt's words) has been fallen back upon too often and too vulgarly, as a substitute for the kind of 'modernisation' which might 'strain people's intellects . . . and undermine unity under accustomed leaders'. The unwritten essence of the eighteenth century has been worn down into today's hollow shell of identity – 'the way we do things' in order to avoid a constitution which might risk making the British normal, or like everybody else.

6   HAIR-SHIRT BRITISHNESS

Slowly the poison the whole blood stream fills.
It is not the effort nor the failure tires.
The waste remains, the waste remains and kills.

It is not your system or clear sight that mills
Down small to the consequence a life requires;
Slowly the poison the whole blood stream fills.

William Empson, 'Missing dates'
(1937) in *Complete Poems* (Allen Lane 2000)

The population retains the periodic power to evict a government, nat-urally, as in 1979 and 1997. But this can now occur only when popular loathing has attained seismic or vomiting level. It no longer has much to do with policies or calculations of interest. In between such spasms, all that Westminster 'representatives' can do is inflict another session of 'Britain', this weird no-man's-land upon which the old undergoes daily humiliation, as the New fails to be politically born. Constant ideological assault and battery makes those half-represented half-believe that every-thing is changing utterly – *and* at the same time, continuing pretty much as it always has done. Gradual evolution used to be the British way; the 'British' one that has replaced it both parrots and exaggerates the rhetoric of gradualism, the better to conceal its jolting disintegration, and a collapse into ever lower circles of descent. The result is that weird *faute-de-mieux* existence I tried to describe earlier: business-as-usual, conducted on an escalator of ignominy and shame.

British society – or 'civil society' in the current jargon – is of course anything but *faute-de-mieux*. A recent report from the Demos research unit confirmed the strange contrast in the working-class new town of Basildon, Essex. The Basildonians voted New Labour in 1997, but now 'see their own prospects for self-improvement as good, but not the future of society as a whole'. This divorce between private and public has become even more drastic since 1997 than under the Thatcher–Major régime, to the point where 'political parties are failing to capture the hearts and minds of Basildon's voters' (*Basildon: the Mood of the Nation*, March 2001).

But this just means that a different, helplessly unplanned country has emerged, and most people really know it, notably in places like Basildon New Town. An actually renewed 'little England' has *of course* arisen, and is lived out day by day, a lot of the time quite cheerfully. British 'civil society' has indeed advanced, and become in many ways almost incredibly better, and better-off. No one who endured the 1950s (for instance) can fail to recall with a shudder just how much worse everyday living then was, for nearly everybody. But the British countries have been little different in this respect from most others in the industrialised world of the post-World War II boom and 'golden age'. The United Kingdom has of course lost its erstwhile dominance, but retained a relatively favourable status, albeit now heavily biased towards places like Basildon New Town and the 'Roseland' circle. Gross inequalities have increased, both social and territorial. However, most individuals have found themselves on the 'better-off' side of these divides. To deplore the UK political system and state tradition in no way entails a denial of such self-evident facts.

What it does entail is something else – recognition that *just because of this progress*, England–Britain now needs a reconstituted and more democratic state to express it. It needs a new arena of public expression, in which different parties or movements – social, regional, national – could find new feet in such an altered world. Without that, how can such forces make the alliances for a new time, and find the voices for whatever ideas this new society is generating? The point is that these would-be citizens, the 'Youthful Britain' Blairites made so much of after 1997, are prevented from imagining anything like this by the unrelenting pressures of an archaic State, and of the media complex which serves it. In that sense, the overall impact of Redemption politics has been to foster a deepening gulf between society and state, between the private and the public. Thatcherism created the latter, and New Labour has widened it into an abyss.

Again, history is important here. The essence of imperial Britain was an unusually intimate 'fit' between society and state, sustained through a partly hereditary class. The British 'prefects' who dominated civil society (including the economy) also controlled the state. That was the Burkean configuration, the style of unity which broke down irretrievably from the sixties onwards, and has now almost vanished. There is no call whatever to lament this. However, no modern democratic constitution was to take its place. Instead, Old Corruption has been sedulously preserved in the special apartments of Westminster – 'Hogwarts-on-Thames' as John Morrison calls it – where it has gone mad, like Mrs Heathcliff in *Wuthering Heights*.

Since 1997 'reform' has mainly taken the form of Devolution – a trial-and-error *bricolage* of three regional formulae which, however admirable in themselves, were supposed to prop up an unchanged (indeed 're-inforced') Centre. The longer-term result is a disarticulated polity, where Mrs Heathcliff finds herself compelled to reproduce 'tradition' in ever more berserk forms, *in order to avoid replacing it*. 'Britain' must be saved – which means, the maimed kernel of a former hegemony must now be replicated, but with its defective DNA worse each time round. The Winter of Discontent is fast falling into a generation of discontent – a proudly-worn hair-shirt national identity, devoted to rejuvenation rather than a change of wardrobe. This 'Britishness' is marooned in time, and still unshakeably addicted to what the French call '*le grand large*' – the wider maritime–commercial world of its inception, now infused with neo-liberalism and American dominance.

Any analysis which depicts such a machinery of downfall or crisis prompts the question: 'But was it really inevitable?' Collapse surely cannot be fated or predetermined, however difficult it has proved to make new starts? In the case of 'Britain', the answer is straighforward. Of course nothing here was 'fated' in any astrological sense; but so far, McKibbin's 'deeper attachments' to the 'inherited political and constitutional structure' have simply proved too strong for political escape to be possible. Escape-plans have never been lacking; but the inheritance has also evolved mechanisms of occlusion and marginalisation which (with much media help) hold all such plans in limbo. No less is expected of a 'Free country' (etc.).

The previous history of the United Kingdom bestowed unusual power on its media. These have become crazily centralised and coarsened, roughly in tempo with the old state's downfall. Originally a 'nation of newspaper readers', Britain was by 1940 a nation of wireless-listeners and then, as soon as technology allowed, of television-addicts. Monolingual literacy, relatively small size and compacted élite rule all favoured the growth of media influence. The result was a curious civil-society 'totali-tarianism', distinct from formal or bureaucratic control. It relied upon a fostered 'climate' rather than on ideological prescription – thought-Prefects rather than thought-policemen and judges. When George Orwell's *1984* first appeared, Isaac Deutscher at once pointed out how it reflected Britain far more accurately than the Eastern Communism at which it was aimed.

But if *1984* and 'Winston Smith' referred to Britain, then of course today's TV *Big Brother* and *The Weakest Link* stand for Thatcher–Blair-land. Such unwitting caricatures have indeed gained more international fame than Orwell's did half a century ago. The formula has been eagerly imitated abroad – notably by US television – in the name of universal sado-masochism and paranoia. The historical British culture described above was remarkable for its cohesion, and for the cross-class fusion of ideas mobilised as 'Britishness'. It was that inheritance which made Stuart Hall's 'populist idiom' possible after 1979 – and then Blair's more hysterical version after 1997. But the post '79 conjuncture has transformed it into *claustrophobia*. One result was the airless *huis clos* of 2001, an 'election' from which so many felt they had to stand apart, simply to keep breathing. The author Robert Harris (a Labour supporter and friend of Peter Mandelson's) put it very well a few days before the 7th of June:

> Shorn of ideology, cosying up to business, untrammelled by parliament, ultra-centralized, backed up by big money and most of the media, it will bear no resemblance to any left-wing administration in our history. Faced with this much power, what else should a writer display except 'detached disdain'?[41]

The civilizational message radiated by *Big Brother* and *The Weakest Link* is of course somewhat different from the one planned for the Greenwich Millennium Dome. It springs from beyond the Pale – from British realities rather than state aspiration. Oneness of national soul, the 'white glow', has contracted into terroristic browbeating upon Hailsham's darkling plain, where every wicket-gate now carries a sign: '*Keep Out*: Foot & Mouth

---

41 'Tory defeat Good, Labour Stranglehold Chilling', *Sunday Times*, 3 June 2001. Harris's well-known novels include evocations of the late-Hitler Germany which might have won World War II, of the return of Stalinism to post-Cold War Russia, and (perhaps most tellingly of all) of the British 1940s élite which manned the Bletchley Park codebreaking centre – *Enigma* (Arrow 1996).

Disease'. On the horizon we see the lurid glow of the 'City of Destruction' (London). As Harris says, grovelling before its 'shapers of opinion' was a crucial part of New Labour's 2001 election strategy.

State-nations are created from above, and part of that involved shaping opinion over a number of generations. But their institutions can become like nature, and compensate for an absence or variety of national foundations by the energetic deployment of both military and ideal force. Media dictatorship is just part of that 'British' nature. The disappearance of Empire has been replaced by its institutional compound of nostalgia, Monarchy and 'wider-world' commercialism, hysterically re-cycled by politicians and London media-pundits who (correctly) now identify their own life-chances with 'this great Constitution of ours' (etc.). They see their percentage in the lowest common denominator, not in democracy; in corporate rather than reforming populism; and hence in a comfortably decaying state rather than some possibly awkward new constitution.

Today, no 'British' leadership can avoid perceiving 'globalisation' as some sort of continuity with (hence justification of) this past. An affectation of the postmodern thus becomes its excuse for retention of the pre-modern. The step is then a short one to perceiving the chance of re-insertion and of enhanced development along terribly familiar lines. Like French Foreign Minister Hubert Védrine looking ahead for the French (see below), all it sees is a somewhat stronger hand of cards for the Brits to play at the hour of globalisation. Naturally, London will play its hand differently from Paris: the UK's external orientation and financial emphasis – *le grand large* – demands above all trans-oceanic reference and support, via both the remaining Commonwealth traditions and (now more important) the 'Special Relationship'. Relationship (that is) with whoever attains office in the United States, thanks to the slightly less archaic system bequeathed by the American Revolution and Civil War. As we saw earlier, the Euro-currency is only one option within the spectrum – splendid if it props up greatness, discardable if not. Britain's 'national interest' must retain supranational robes – but not necessarily *this* supranationality.

Great Britain's inherited state-form and identity were the products of an Unwritten Constitution derived from the 1688–1707 period. The 'ethnicity' of Great Britain always lay here, and here alone. It is the indwelling *Geist* which compels Redemptive politics to move instinctively along the inherited twin tracks of Westminster archaism and overseas posturing – the inseparable ghouls of a thoroughly decayed early-modern nationalism. To introduce serious central constitutional reform, like the written statutes the Charter 88 movement has been calling for since the eighties, is still seen as implying a kind of needless surrender. It would mean 'becoming like everybody else'. This would bring in train proportional representation, coalition governments, new political parties, the serious arousal of 'Little England', and a focus upon mid-range social and economic policies – the kind of boring stuff which preoccupies politicians in Sweden, Ireland or the Czech Republic. It might be quite popular in Basildon too, if given a chance.

One of the most telling accounts of the deeper mentality of 'Britishness' has been provided by John Morrison in his admirable study *Reforming Britain* (2000). His subtitle is *New Labour, New Constitution* and he relates in an introductory chapter how the Labour Party leadership toyed with proposals for a written British Constitution over the five years following their defeat by John Major's Conservatives in 1992. That defeat badly demoralised them. For some time, they were confronted with the sombre possibility of Labour never returning to office in their own lifetimes. The assumption had been that the 1990 coup against Thatcher and her replacement by a nonentity would almost automatically return the Opposition to government. When this failed to happen, it became evident that something more basic was wrong.

Eventually this anxiety led towards Tony Blair and the Third Way. But for some time it also suggested to the more thoughtful among them that there *might* be something structurally amiss with the British state and Constitution – that fundamental reform could be required simply as a way of restoring 'fairness' to the system. Since 1988, the Charter 88 movement had indeed been agitating in just this direction, and urging proportional representation and Devolution, alongside a formalised apparatus of rights and citizenship. Relatively abruptly, the Charter found itself supported and sympathised with by a Labourite clientele, until then mainly quite indifferent to their cause. John Smith and Gordon Brown found time to address Charterist meetings. There was a new openness to the idea of alliances with the Liberal Democrats and civil society bodies like the Scottish Constitutional Convention, a 'Centre–Left' coalition of ideas and forces that might foster a more effective opposition than Labour had been able to do on its own.

John Morrison's retrospect of this period shows the seriousness of all these overtures, addresses, pamphlets and conferences *at the time.* No one should convict Smith, Brown or the others of mere unprincipled hypocrisy. And yet, in the longer arc of what became Blair's New Labour credo and régime, that is exactly what it now looks like. Just as Lord Hailsham was perfectly sincere in his gloomy prophecy of 'elective dictatorship in 1978–79, and then elated by the 'recovery' of Mrs Thatcher's triumph in May 1979 – so the New Labour reformers were 'brought to their senses' by New Labour's *revanche* of 1997. Hailsham had dreaded a Left tyranny, Smith and the others a long-term Right hegemony. Both thought in party terms, not state or national ones. And for both, all was well again once the old system abruptly reasserted its primitive force.

For the Blairites what made this aspect of the earlier 'Blair Project' instant history was of course the 'overwhelming' 1997 result. An excited Redemptionism at once invaded every tissue of the ancient polity, firing new life into Crown and festering Northern pocket-burgh alike. It is true that the whole world was made aware of profound agitations within the old Kingdom, after Princess Diana died in the late summer of 1997. This event abruptly cast a shadow of mortality upon the Monarchy which had expelled her. A different social nation briefly flourished in the streets. It seemed to be searching for both the lost soul and the fantasy alternative royalty the Princess had been felt to embody. Whatever the embryo society was seeking will never be known, however, since the state brought down the shutters on it.

Blair's New Labour simply sent for the plumbers. Such philistine brusqueness is explained by unease. After all, one alternative might then have led to others, posed tiresome constitutional problems, and taken the gilt off their recent triumph. The New Labour Party was seeking gratitude and conformity from its public, not bad verse and heartfelt aspirations. So the unquiet grave was briskly filled in, the Royal waxworks were eased back into place, and given appropriate things to say. Lessons in philistinism ('modernization') were solemnly dispensed from every forum. The Windsors had to pull their socks up, so that the *real problems* might be proceeded with.

Central constitutional change is not really resisted in Ukania because it is 'boring' or unwanted by Middle England. With comparatively little effort the public-relations apparatus now at the disposal of UK governments could make it a key part of 'modernisation', rejuvenation (and so on). It is refused because this might mean an identity-switch: dropping the national narratives of the British keystone, greatness and leadership. Not knowing quite which 'Britain' it is to stand up for, the politico-cultural élite would lose its adrenalin overnight. It would find itself merely in charge, rather than in command, of a pretty ordinary collection of archipelago lands. Rational counter-pressures would start to build up inside the system, rather than in exile from it, and find expression through alliances and negotiation – the very process which New Labour was moving towards in the nineties, when it was feared inevitable. There might then be little point in (for example) keeping the Pound Sterling, and none whatever in retaining the Nuclear Deterrent, or in sacrificing what remains of manufacturing to make sure the City can continue surfing the (supposed) waves of globalisation. One could simply forget about leading 'Europe', resign from the Security Council, and cease clinging so portentously to the coattails of the US Presidency.

7   CONSTITUTIONAL ARTHRITIS

To strengthen Parliament in fulfilling its functions is to boost the health of the political system. That is our starting point . . . We accept the basic attributes of the Westminster model . . . Our task therefore is not to create a new constitutional framework for the United Kingdom but rather to ensure that the balance within the Westminster system is achieved.

Philip Norton, Report for William Hague,
Strengthening Parliament, as quoted in John Morrison,
'Hogwarts-on-Thames', *Reforming Britain: New Labour,
New Constitution?* (Reuters 2001)

In Ukania, when any new-age party politico utters the words 'real problems', dirty ideological work is afoot. A rise of 75 pence per week for the pensioners or a cut in the interest rate elide seamlessly into the supposed meaning of some governmental 'package'. This package is essential to 'Britain' becoming herself again. Thus small bribes and the matter of Sovereignty compose a still-seamless whole. Within that whole, 'balance' is everything. Mild loss of equilibrium is all that can go wrong with such a wonderful old clock. The jargon for this kind of trick is 'joined-up thinking', as described in *Chairman Blair's Little Red Book* (Steve Bell and Brian Homer, 2000):

> Joined-up thinking is the ability to merge disparate concepts into one significant big idea ... It has been proved that intelligence can be an impediment to joined-up thinking. It is essential when engaging in joined-up thinking always to apply Chairman Blair's thoughts ... (p. 135)

These thoughts invariably extend seamlessness back into anterior time – that of the gradual, infinitely adaptable powers of the most wondrous of human Constitutions. Lacking a humdrum ethnic foundation, 'Britain' compensates with clockwork: supernatural civic powers, the Providentially prescribed powers of Crown and Parliament. The womb of time stands ever open, revealing its unshakeable control over all Britons yet to be.

All Britannic subjects stumble across this mystic inheritance several times per day. I know a Sunderland pensioner who possesses a complete collection of Royal Souvenir mugs, from 1922 down to the present. The 1922 souvenir is the most interesting, a pewter ashtray showing an embossed portrait of the young Prince of Wales (subsequently Edward VIII). He is wearing a naval cap at a rakish angle, and has a cigarette dangling prominently from his lower lip. The inscription reads 'Our Prince of Sports' – a vivid reminder of how, after the travails of 1914–18 (and just as the Irish Free State was being born), the British Crown was already busy 'modernising', and preparing to become the emblem of a rejuvenated country. Recently all the items had to be taken down and dusted when a new carpet was laid, and I noticed they had been replaced with a space at one end. 'For Charles and Camilla?' I inquired. '*No!*' came the reply, which I felt to be a trifle brisk – 'it's for when Prince William gets married, and *sorts all that lot out*'.

'Real problems' – public sector miseries, non-arriving trains, leaking roofs, sink estates and overflowing prisons – are conjured away by the joined-up sensibility, and set ultimately within a Regal frame. The transcendent realm is returning to its seventeenth-century origins in another way also. As we saw above, it has increasingly Christian, or neo-Christian, overtones to it. On 8 May 2001 Prime Minister Blair's public announcement (mentioned above) turned Ukania into something like an Evangelical meeting. This preacherly populism struck the keynote of the ensuing campaign – presumably as another way of countering 'apathy'. But that was only possible in a climate already prepared by the Prime Minister's outspoken personal Christianity, and his consistent endorsement of spectral 'community'. As Anne McElvoy put it, under Blair 'community' is constantly nigh, often in offensively new garb:

> It exudes a kind of vague, well-meaning buzz associated (e.g.) with Robert Putnam's guest appearance at a No. 10 seminar as communitarian of the moment. All due respect to Putnam as a thinker, but there is something a bit over-familiar about this latest fascination. Remember Amitai Etzioni? Will Hutton's Stakeholding? Communitarians are the buses in the Blair years. Miss one and there's another rolling along behind. (*Independent* 4 April 2001)

But the buses have taken all passengers on to the same destination: the 'British' terminus of indurate custom and the backward glance. Glimpses are permitted of other vistas from the community-bus windows, but one may alight only within the wondrous mechanism, the oldest constitution (and so on). As R.W. Johnson has pointed out in a recent *London Review of Books* article (5 July 2001), the 'constitutional revolution' so loudly trumpeted by Blairism has underscored this inevitability like nothing else. It is the 1997 régime's greatest achievement by far – but also, the change most revelatory of the futility of twenty-first-century 'Britain'.

Mrs Thatcher felt that Moses had inspired every quirk of British Constitutionalism, and would tolerate no change at all. Blair and Brown are broader-minded: they do think some changes are needed to 'modernise' Constitutionalism. But of course this is Prince of Wales modernisation. It means *strengthening*, improvement – restart rather than new start. It implies 'marrying the century one is living in', in General de Gaulle's phrase. As with French decentralisation, UK 'Devolution' was aimed at augmenting central authority by rationalising it. It was not a surrender of sovereignty, or the severance of ties. As Ministers have constantly reiterated, it was directed towards the *suppression* of the nationalist impulses that had begun to show themselves in Scotland, Wales and Northern Ireland from the sixties onwards.

The view from Mrs Heathcliff's tower is that such peripheral restlessness may always be assuaged by reasonable concessions. The criteria of 'reason' are well known to all those in both tower and drawing-room. Has not the long process of Centre-of-Things civilisation defined them, and demonstrated their superiority? Like Indirect Rule before it, Responsible regional self-government was a thoroughly good thing. And it was quite distinct from – indeed thoroughly opposed to – irresponsible nationalism. From the sixties onwards, reorganising local government had been an *idée fixe* of all UK governments. This really derived from the absolute unthinkability of changing the head, or central authority-system. By contrast, it always seemed at once easy and terribly modern to have one's way with the executive limbs. The Unwritten Mystery could be left in peace, while the 'grass roots' were galvanised – the agencies and personnel of the local governments, so wisely devoted to the 'real problems' of subjects. What was 'Devolution' but a natural extension of this trend? Once awarded, reasonable people among the national minorities would then gratefully reaffirm their loyalty to central power, thus enhancing the UK's standing and clout.

As for 'the others' (malcontents bent upon shedding Union tutelage) both Dr Reid and the First Minister of devolved Scotland, the late Donald Dewar, constantly said that New Labour's smart move would *kill separatism stone dead*. Note the overwhelming train of thought here. It was confidently predicted that Scottish nationalism (for instance), after emerging from virtual oblivion in the 1960s to being a near majority in the 1990s, would not simply be contained or politically defeated: it had to *disappear*. Those Scots who despaired of the United Kingdom (usually on social democratic grounds) and wanted to join Europe on their own account, or get into the Nordic Union, were not just consigned to opposition. They were to curl up and die. Note also where the tone of savagery and dismissal lies in this spectrum: not in the ranks of the Scottish National Party or Plaid Cymru, but *on the British side* – and uttered in this case by Scots.

The second-term New Labour government is reputedly envisaging a general 'Secretary of State for Devolution', as replacement for the old Secretaries of State for Scotland, Wales and Northern Ireland. These Ministers have of course been under-employed since the appearance of elected assemblies, so what could be more logical than a 'Czar' (the term has become current since 1997) for the periphery? The Czar of the Regions would in fact be a Secretary for stone-dead stage-exits, Regional Reason and the re-education of repentant Separatists. Dr Reid is rumoured to have his eye on this job, for which he is indeed thoroughly qualified. As Blairism has inadvertently shown, charisma and 'community' alone are now unlikely to save the Crown. The Centre cannot hold without a good deal more ruthless management, supine committees and adroit vote-fixing – traditional 'bourgeois politics' (as Marxists used to say), but in Ukania most ably cultivated by the Old Labour Party.

'New Labour's sheer lack of coherence is nowhere more striking than when one looks at its greatest achievement, constitutional reform', comments R.W. Johnson in the same article. The decision to devolve power to the smaller countries of the Union was made (necessarily) *without* a preparatory or analogous reform of the 1688–1707 antiques. It was carried out partly for party motives, and partly as a saving 'compromise' against peripheral nationalism. Its success demanded that Little England stay little, and if possible decently hidden in the shrubbery, until the British glow could shine forth more strongly again.

Over the same period as Devolution was permitted, England-without-Britain was informally re-baptised. During the later 1990s it became 'Middle England': a faithful heartland of good souls and *Daily Mail* readers, bored by constitutional nonsense, happy with the old theatre, sceptical about the 'extra layers of government' which (e.g.) any new English or English-regional set-up would surely have brought. Through the transformist miracle New Labour had conquered this land, Southern or London's England, the Home Counties (as they used to be labelled). The 2001 election was essentially a reaffirmation of that victory, permitting the *parvenus* of 1997 to settle more comfortably into long-term ownership.

The result was a system born decrepit. In the not-so-long run this shrivelled babe was bound to amplify the instability already inherent in two-party redemptionism. Devolution was meant to consolidate the system by allowing a harmless quantity of 'voice'; but voice can lead towards 'exit' unless broader, more plural parameters are established at the same time. In this case the purpose was to avoid such parameters. The lone exception was the British-Irish Council linked to the Belfast Agreement – but it has turned out to be a fantasy detour, the short-lived guilt-trip of elective dictatorship, possible only when an exceptionally large spread of opinion-formers had to be fooled, all at one time. As Johnson concludes:

> The whole constitutional construction is jerry-built, riven by contradic-
> tions at every level and thus unstable ... If New Labour really was 'a
> party of principle' it would have started by recognising that you can't
> have constitutional reform without first having a written constitution.

The 'principle' which was actually operating here has confirmed its tenth-
rateness by the House of Lords farce. Blair and Brown's 'Radicalism' could
not even put an end to Lordship, never mind the Monarchy. The Lords
have ended up rather like the Crown: 'modernised', and brought more
securely into the ambit of committee-land, vote-purchase and moral assas-
sination. It is clearly felt that Ukania could no longer even pretend to be
herself without this abysmal facsimile of tradition.

In a time now forgotten, a former style of radicalism used to decry the
British state's 'illogicality'. But today's successors are now confident enough
to defend the trope: after all, should logic really be required of a 'world
power' on such matters? There is another way, with a greater echo of true
lordship to it. May not insouciance over piffling matters be a way of
demonstrating the profounder self-confidence at work: the thousand years
lying ahead (as well as behind)? Consistency, by contrast, is for dogmatic
pipsqueaks, 'micro-states' which boringly try to mean what they say, quite
often through the proportional representation of their electorates, and
hopelessly indecisive coalition governments.

Given the chance (admittedly somewhat limited), how have the three
new peripheral governments of the United Kingdom all chosen to move?
In precisely this hopeless direction. They have been helped by the preposterous and entirely characteristic mistake made by the UK statesmen and
advisors who prepared the Devolution legislation. Sincerely convinced
after 1997 that democracy would enfeeble Britain, all bauble-bearing medi-
ocrities were forced to perceive the procedure as highly commendable *for
the regions*. Surely, allowing proportional representation in Northern

Ireland, Wales and Scotland would *prevent* strong, assertive governments from emerging there? A bit illogical, perhaps; but it did mean that nationalists were unlikely ever to gain 'commanding majorities'. No Plaid Cymru or SNP government would (for example) ever conquer an overwhelming majority with 25 per cent of the vote. Instead, 'PR' would ensure they found themselves forever bogged down in compromises with representatives of the reasonable (or British-minded) majorities there.

Thus did bankruptcy's cheap cunning win the day. However, nascent democracy has at least been able to seize upon its mistake, and set about constructing alternatives. It is striking how, behind and after this happy error of 1997, a boundless central complacency still prevails. The mistake was not only about the superstructures of Britain: an appraisal of the English themselves was also involved. The latter were deemed to be 'by nature' (not just the second nature of imperialism) unconcerned about matters of small-land identity, or arcane questions of constitutionalism. They were seen as forever dwelling in Anglo-Britain, and (hence) as remaining like Play-Doh in the hands of one or other Westminster élite. Since the majority of Scots, Welsh and Northern Irish have strong personal and family ties with the English – and are in that sense interested in conserving UK civil society and institutions – it was assumed the plasticine-effect would endure out there as well. No mere changes in 'local government' would affect this, surely? Harmless local colour about tradition and past centuries was unlikely to make such sensible folk neglect their 'real problems'.

As Johnson writes, this entire constitutional stance amounted to a house of greasy cards set up on a rickety old table. The house is taking some time to collapse – but only because the same party controls all four governments. In spite of which, four years after the Devolution agreed on for Wales and Scotland, three after the Belfast Agreement in Northern Ireland, these working régimes are moving (when permitted to move at all) in a direction profoundly at variance with Great Britain *redevivus*. Such an aim and tendency is not likely to be limited for long by legislative fiat. These are quite clearly would-be social-democratic governments, beginning to recruit their own support in new ways made possible by the measure of distance which Devolution (in spite of itself) has established for them.

8   THE WATCHDOGS

It is evident what a distastefully heterogeneous mixture the character of the British Whigs must turn out to be: Feudalists who are at the same time Malthusians, money-mongers with feudal prejudices, aristocrats without points of honour, Bourgeois with no industrial activity, finality-men with progressive phrases, progressists with fanatical Conservatism, traffickers in homeopathical fractions of reform, fosterers of family nepotism, Grand Masters of corruption, hypocrites of religion, the Tartuffes of politics . . .

Karl Marx, 'The Elections in England – Tories and Whigs',
New York Daily Tribune, 21 August 1852

For 'Whigs' read 'New Labour'. But since the homeopathical fractions of devolutionary medicine look like recoiling upon its dispensers, somewhat sterner measures are needed. The 'Council of the Isles' was like a homeopathical festival, followed by a return to real medicine: splints, surgery and cough-mixtures. In theory, the conclusion of the Devolution 'process' could be what is prefigured in Norman Davies' recent survey of off-shore history, *The Isles*: a de-unitarised archipelago, or a confederation of polities, including England – whether as 'little England' or as an assemblage of regions. This would not be too unlike the conception animating

Jean-Marie Colombani's conception of a future France in *Les infortunes de la République* (discussed below). The 'misfortunes' of both states arise from contradictions between eighteenth-century shells and the new life-contents emerging after the Cold War. The Scottish National Party's long-established formula for such a future is an 'Association of British States'.

But here, as in France, such notions now encounter an army of determined reactionary opinion. 'Britain' may be in poor shape, but its institutional apparatus of political and administrative watchdogs can still put up a fight, and still commands plenty of resources. A 'Save the Union' movement has long been in formation in the UK, and appears likely to assume more ostentatious forms, as New Labour failure and demoralisation take their course.

Among the assets of British retro-nationalism are the cadres of state, a substantial part of the intelligentsia, most of the media, and the personal goodwill of one nationality towards another I mentioned previously – still widespread in the archipelago. There is also an important *sui generis* body of popular opinion in Northern Ireland, among Ulster Protestants. The latter are devoted less to the faltering Britishness of the present, than to an imagined past of imperial blood and iron. Another crucial sector of opinion is that of the immigrant minorities (largely in England). Although not 'pro-British' in the old-Unionist sense, recent immigrants remain hesitant about opposing it, for fear of 'something worse'. And this allows retro-nationalism some house-room among them.

Another useful watchdog is the extraordinarily low historical profile of constitutional reform in Britain. This does not apply at all in France, where in the past political crises have given a permanent salience to constitutional formality, and to the definition of citizenship. In Ukania constitutionalism has begun to assert itself in earnest only through the problems and after-effects of Devolution. But so far it has not yet gained enough ground to challenge the current New Labour slide back into Unwritten reverence, preservative helmsmanship and modernised Monarchy.

New Labour's second term in office, from 2001 to (probably) 2004 or 2005, looks likely to deepen and sanctify this reactionary fall-back. Observers have often noted how the 'campaign' for Blair's return to office started up on 2 May 1997, the day following his 'landslide' triumph. The same happened again in 2001, in farther emulation of Mrs Thatcher's extended era of power. As landslide turns in stages towards incipient débâcle, possibly aggravated by economic recession, party and media will tend to lose faith in Blair himself and – still unable to 'strain people's intellects . . . and undermine unity' with constitutional change – search for alternative leadership. Chancellor Brown is still the most quoted candidate, for quite evident reasons. Blair may be the true 'Dr Britain' (see below); but the Iron Chancellor may yet be – or at least aspire to be – Saviour of the Union'.

It was Brown's adroit footwork which produced the new alignment between UK capitalism and Labour government immediately following the 1997 election, and so removed the old bone of contention between the Treasury and the City. By awarding control of interest rates to the latter, he ensured his government would benefit from the continuing conditions of trade expansion that marked the whole 1997–2001 period. The cost of this was abandonment of Labour's former policy of weak-kneed support and subsidy for British manufacturing and extractive industry – effectively, a final capitulation to the commercial and financial interests of the City. But as a historian, Brown knew very well how futile and inconsequent such support had always been. He must have calculated that surrender was the better bet.

Another result of that shift was to make New Labour much more decisively a party of the English South: as I noted before, 'Middle England' became the euphemism for this, an adjustment towards heartland norms (actual or imagined) which entailed some withdrawal from the Labour Party's old power-base in the North and the periphery. Swimming with the tide, instead of floundering ineffectually against it, promised a more solid hegemony. However, this mutation had to be 'covered' and justified for such a route-change to work: put more crudely, the North had to be given time to die off decently, while the New Labour authority-structure put down more durable roots in the formerly Tory South.

I noted earlier the strong support for simple-majority elections, in terms of imagined 'Sovereignty', overwhelmingness, the accoutrements of Greatness and institutional Nostalgia. But there is another and more sordid reason for clinging to 'first-past-the-post'. The *party* still depends upon it, above all at the level of local government and city politics. Throughout the Northern conurbations (including the Scottish indus-trial belt) Labourism had long been a 'one-party state' thanks to its control and manipulation of the old electoral order.[42] That dominance was incom-patible with proportionality, or (as London was to show) with the direct election of Mayors. And the fact that these areas are now in retreat (partly on orders from Westminster) does not lessen the importance of Labourite control. Eventually the City-led strategy of post-industrialism will pre-sumably bring a graveyard quietus to these ex-industrial zones. Until then, however – while New Labour's successor-Britain is finding its feet – it is if

---

42 In one of the most telling surveys of Labour support to appear before the 2001 elec-tion, Ivor Crewe showed just how strongly the system now favours the party in power. Since the mid-1990s 'the electoral system has been strongly biased in favour of Labour . . . delivering considerably more seats to Labour than to the Conservatives for the same share of the national vote'. This is partly because of support from Scotland and Wales, and partly through Labour control of 'de-populating industrial and inner-city areas', mainly in the North. It follows that New Labour will use every means available to preserve such an advantage, by cultivating 'Old Labour' local corruption in its traditional fiefdoms. See 'The pro-Labour bias of the electoral system', in Chapter 4, *The Blair Effect: The Blair Government 1997–2001*, edited by Anthony Seldon (Little, Brown 2001).

anything more essential that Old Labour plays its servile part, by staying loyally in charge of 'the North.'

That New Labour rests so totally upon Old Labour corruption may appear another of R.W. Johnson's régime 'contradictions'. And so it is; but this is what watchdogs are for. Think-tanks and nebulous idea-projectionists have of course become invaluable servants of Redemption. However, they alone cannot make things stick. The unspeakable also requires plumbers and drain-clearers – agents of despatch and delivery, capable of pushing things through. Brown's centrality to the Project is the way that he (unlike Blair) conjoins a smartly ignominious broad strategy with deep sensitivity to the needs of his party mafiosi. Unlike Blair, he is a 'man of the Party', as well as of the Union. The steeds of the Undead come together naturally in his reins. Could there be a better Leader of reaction, once Project-impetus has slackened, resources have to be mobilised and enemies rounded upon?

The most penetrating commentary on this side of a potential Brown leadership has come from Gerry Hassan and Jim McCormick. In their article 'Blair: the Future of Britain and the Britishness', it is suggested that in the original 1994 agreement between Blair and Brown, which led to the former becoming uncontested Leader, Brown was 'given Scotland'.[43] He had become uncomfortably aware that many Scottish MPs might not support him in a vote, and was 'compensated' with a free hand in the fiefdom. One part of the deal was Devolution itself – something which Brown had strongly supported since the days of the *Red Paper on Scotland* (1975). But the implication was also that, once devolved, Scottish politics were to be

---

43 *Soundings* Review, August 2001. A more extensive analysis can be found in *Tomorrow's Scotland*, edited by G. Hassan and C. Warhurst (Lawrence & Wishart 2002 forthcoming), the most important overview of Scottish politics since Devolution in 1997.

Brown's preserve – somewhat as Poland was carved up between Ribbentrop and Molotov in 1939, the authors suggest. The consequence has been a situation different from any previously known – an occluded dictatorship under which Brown has intervened at every level, including 'influencing the selection of candidates personally, or trying to stop an open, democratic election for the post of First Minister' after Donald Dewar's death. Their verdict is that 'Brown's feudal treatment of Scottish politics is the desperate act of a passing old order' and exhibits 'a very limited, Westminster kind of politics which shows the parameters of the "new Unionism"'.

The stage-settings for Brownite Scotland are thus related to the others mentioned above. Another vital parameter lay in a crucial first-term victory of the old Guard: the subordination of the Liberal Democrats. The great zombie come-back of June 2001 was enabled by a systemic prostration of the main centre-ground party. After 1997 Paddy Ashdown's party was kept 'on-side' by specious assurances about this 'centre-left' common ground and an eventual, possible, timely, thoroughly-considered (and of course popularly-ratified) change to the way Britishers vote. In the period 1996–97 (when the Blairites were anything but confident of outright victory) we saw how quite a different tone prevailed. The possibility had then to be envisaged of a 'progressive' alliance with the Liberal Democrats, in case this turned out to be the sole avenue to office. Paddy Ashdown's Liberal-Democrat party had been demanding electoral reform for decades, as a precondition of government – and also, as an opening towards wider constitutional changes, including even a 'federal' structure for the United Kingdom. Any such alliance would have rendered some central shifts unavoidable – that is, shifts towards democracy and the 'normalisation' of both constitution and administration. 'Devolution' might then have had more principle built into it, and resembled more closely (for example) the systems already functioning in Spain, Belgium or Germany.

In the most balanced assessment of Blair's government so far, *Did Things Get Better?* by Polly Toynbee and David Walker (Penguin 2001), it is noticeable how this fundamental failure is presented. The authors admit how hard it is to draw up a balance-sheet in terms of policies alone. They point out that in so many areas the picture has been one of hyperactivity yielding indeterminate results which (as in conventional House of Commons debates) can be 'read both ways'. By contrast, the strategic architecture of New Labour's first government leaves them no room for doubt. The objective of constitutional change via a long-term alliance with other centre-left forces had seemed initially to be *the* most important element of 'the Project'. It alone would 'make the twenty-first century safe for progressive forces'. In spite of their general support for New Labour, Toynbee and Walker are force to concede that this did not merely fail. *It was junked* (p. 238).

Worse than that, the Liberal Democrats found themselves unable to rebel against their fate. The supreme insult came in the run-up to the 2001 Pantomine, when Blair solemnly announced that the Project was not dead, merely in hibernation. Like joining the Euro-currency, it lay somewhere up ahead, in the haze of . . . 2003. A referendum *might* quite possibly be held then or later, on the weakest conceivable form of proportional representation. This might not be successful (given that a majority of New Labour MPs now oppose it). Or, of course, it might just be *junked* once more, in recognition of how little Middle England appears to care for that kind of thing. The new Leader of the Liberal-Democrats, Charles Kennedy, was unable to do other than 'welcome' this blatantly counterfeit pledge, albeit with trembling upper lip and many reservations.

In the middle years of Blair's first term, as the Movement's watchdogs observed events in Scotland, Wales, Northern Ireland and (worst of all) London, an implacable campaign of resistance was swelling up among them to any change of that kind. Sovereignty is bad for Generals, but even more toxic for Lieutenants and the back-bench infantry. Under the leadership of Brown and John Prescott, this has become a classical campaign of reaction. Unionists who have had experience of 'thus far' with Devolution, are if anything now more determined on 'no farther' than was Lady Thatcher back in '79.

The rules of parody-Britain would seem in any case to prescribe a Majorite phase for New Labour. That is, the period of bedraggled exhaustion during which High Office falls back upon steady-as-she-goes, sleaze multiplies, and popular hatred of 'Them' again builds up towards explosion level. However, 2002–2007 will differ from 1992–97 in a number of ways. The delay (and finally the counter-movement) over reform of the state, Devolution, indecision over Europe and the likelihood of economic downturn are all injecting new poisons into an already staggering and inconsequent system. After such a catalogue of atrocious failures and shames, its watchdogs will be forced into sterner counter-actions and reprisals.

Only three weeks after the June election, ominous and concordant accounts of the governmental mindset came from different observers. What they indicated was the utter contrary of what might be expected from a Party and government so strongly vindicated by an election. New Labour had decided on an election, carried it through against considerable difficulties, pulped or sidelined all opposition, and for the first time in the history of British Labourism repeated an earlier 'overwhelming' performance. Years of unassailable power lay before it. Blair now enjoyed even greater authority than Thatcher in mid-career. This is an inherently top-down system, now with a leadership more securely on top than most of its predecessors. So surely some elation and soaring ambition was in order?

The headlines of the accounts mentioned read as follows: 'Be Worried, Mr Blair, be Very, Very Worried' (Peter Riddell, *Times*, 2 July 2001); 'They look so fed up, you wouldn't think they'd just won an election'

(Steve Richards, *Sunday Independent*, 1 July 2001); 'What a bunch of miserable winners!' (Andrew Rawnsley, *Observer*, 1 July 2001). The concordance of views is all the more striking from three writers critical of, but also broadly sympathetic to, New Labour. Even such well-disposed critics could detect little but woe and disillusionment *in the first week* of New Labour's victorious return. Riddell reminds Blair of how few actually voted for him on the 7th of June, and foresees abstention quickly turning to loathing, especially among the young, where we are witnessing:

> a serious disconnection between mainstream politics and working-class voters . . . [who] read newspapers and watch television much less than other groups, while the fragmentation of the mass media means there is no longer any sense of a common national experience from watching the same news programmes.

Richards depicted government re-starting around an ignoble and largely unintelligible row about private sector involvement in the promised improvement of public services like health and education. This was not about specifics at all, he observed, but (like most New Labour arguments) 'over hot air':

> Most sequels begin where the original ended. Labour's second term seems to be beginning where the original began, with rows over vacuous words rather than actual policies. No wonder Labour MPs are looking gloomy. They have no idea what *precisely* they should be feeling gloomy about.

Rawnsley paints an even more deperate picture. In *this* new dawn it is practically suicidal to be alive, and among the ranks of the elect. 'The second term has not been launched, it has plopped', he groans, '[t]he massed ranks of Labour MPs were silent, even sullen, as they listened to the Prime Minister . . . It could not be more different from the narcotic atmosphere' of 1997. He is forced back on the Hidden Masterplan hypothesis:

> I guess it is possible that there is a secret masterplan locked up in a safe at No. 10 Downing Street. There had better be. Because the main impression given by the government is that it doesn't have much of a clue about what it really wants to do with its second term.

In this Stygian-dark panorama, even Gordon Brown's announcement that he is in no hurry to join the European currency ranks as 'a significant contribution'. 'Bizarre isn't the word for it', concludes Rawnsley.

I suspect the word for it is 'British'. This is Britain, nor are we out of it. Indeed we are in some ways deeper in it than before the 7th of June. No euphoric fuss is being worked up in the election's wake, because none is necessary. In A.J.P. Taylor's famous phrase, the purpose of Hapsburg government was to go on existing in as much grandeur as could still be mustered; and Windsor-Westminsterdom is in the same plight. Return again to Bulpitt's terse overview, quoted earlier: 'these structural characteristics have produced party élites with common, initial, subsistence-level objectives, namely winning national office, avoiding too many problems while there and getting re-elected. Any other objectives are jam on the bread . . .'. All that parodic 'Britain' has done is to exaggerate these characteristics, and June 2001 was a notable turn of the screw. The problems – or 'events' – are harder to avoid, more disasastrous when they happen, and there is less and less state 'jam' (save in the form of patronage or, eventually, outright sleaze and corruption). Never have the conditions for pariahdom looked so good.

9 THE INCOMER'S DILEMMA

Britishness, as much as Englishness, has systematic, largely un-
spoken, racial connotations. Whiteness nowhere features as an explicit
condition of being British, but it is widely understood that Englishness,
and therefore by extension Britishness, is racially coded . . . Race is
deeply entwined with political culture and with the idea of nation, and
underpinned by a distinctively British kind of reticence – to take race
and racism seriously, or even to talk about them at all, is bad form,
something not done in polite company. This . . . has proved a lethal
combination.

The Future of Multi-Ethnic Britain: The Parekh Report,
(Runnymede Trust, London 2000), Chapter 3,
'Identities in Transition', pp. 38–9.

Among the more noticeable assets of the Chancellor of the Exchequer
must be counted his nationality. Not only do Scots play a disproportionate part in the New Labour government, they seem certain to have a
leadership role in its reactionary turn, and in the preparations now under
way for the last redoubt. They will without doubt be foremost in any battle
to restrict, or even roll back, the devolved parliaments which many of
them did a great deal to create. Why is this?

It is important to remember a very general point here: the representatives of small (and often repressed) nations have almost invariably played
a significant part in building up greater multinational states. Indeed they
have often given them both voice and political leadership. There is no
particular mystery about this. Immigrants normally have a mixture of

distance from and enterprising curiosity about their host country, which conveys certain advantages. They can perceive and exploit aspects of the new home culture more readily than many natives – for whom this matrix remains taken for granted, a matter for 'instinct' (often incurious) rather than for access and manipulation.

Though clearly important in commerce and business, the immigrant edge probably counts for most among intellectuals – and hence, in modern times, for politics as well. From the seventeenth century onwards an interface developed between ideas and political life, growing especially important during all moments of disruption and rapid change. Revolutions and counter-revolutions were the junctures of choice here – those times when a dislocated or reformed society felt conscious need of different visions and choices. In the formation of Great Britain, this was strikingly true in and following the revolutions of the era 1640–1707 – nor did it cease to hold throughout the eighteenth century. The latter would later be nostalgicised as one of equipoise and stability; but in reality it exhibited (as Karl Marx observed so powerfully) a constant and ruthless upheaval, which in no sense 'settled down' until far into his own nineteenth century.

The shaping influence of Scottish and Irish intellectuals upon that process is one of its most celebrated features. Empiricist philosophy and Political Economy were among their contributions to the evolving British (before long simply 'English') *Weltanschauung*, as in the work of Hume and Adam Smith. After 1789, the most lasting formulation of what it now meant to be 'British' came from the Irishman Edmund Burke. Later, the Welshman David Lloyd-George would become the British Empire's battle-hero of 1915 to 1922. Even in the 1960s it was an Englishman, John Stevenson, who led the resurgence of the IRA's armed struggle under the pseudonym of 'Seán Mac Stiofáin'. Farther afield, the Georgian Joseph Stalin became the chieftain of Russia in its Great Patriotic War; Eamon De Valera was a half-Spanish

American, before he became the Leader of Irish nationalism; the Austrian Adolf Hitler came to believe that he embodied the German Race; and it was a Montenegrin, Slobodan Milosevic, who in the 1990s turned himself into the terrifying spearhead of Great-Serb nationalism.

I mention such familiar facts to remind the reader that the history of transplant Great-nationalism may not yet be extinct. 'Britain' may still be able to count on quite a sturdy transference-effect of the same sort – even though its results are now wildly different, or even opposed to that of so many famed godfathers. Phony 'revolutions' like those of 1979 and 1997 have produced no new ideas. New Ideas are deceitful creatures: they tend to insinuate themselves clandestinely, like thieves in the night, then pounce when no one expects them. On the whole, think-tanks are death to new ideas. However, what nobody can deny is that terminal Britain has shown a lusty appetite for *pseudo-ideas*. Just as (in the time of Edmund Burke) the rise of the British realm was calling for blueprints of advance or experiment, so its current disaggregation has a brought an unslakeable thirst for plausible misconstructions, brazen apologias and the specious parade of business-as-usual in and around the *Bunker*. Defence of the doomed and the unspeakable may lack the dignity of speculation on Progress; but it is obviously quite hard work.

The salience of Scottish and Welsh bagmen among Blair's choristers of Britain can of course also be accounted for quite mundanely. The long shipwreck of the eighties produced a disproportionate number of peripheral cadres, from those regions where Labourism survived better. This led to Welsh then Scottish leadership, under Kinnock and John Smith respectively. When at last New Labour was borne on the 'up' escalator, so were their many disciples and accomplices, including Gordon Brown. The 'inevitability' of Devolution was part of that same trend, favouring the national minorities over representatives of the English North or the newer immigrant communities.

But the *militancy* of the resultant counter-tendency – its unrequitable and aggressive passion for The Union – requires that another dimension be taken into account. When moving in to a host culture, immigrants sense its undiscovered potential – which in former times meant, above all, its potential for general advance or development. Both individual and communal advancement or careerism then found their place within the growth-points of such a perspective. They became a contribution to the eclosion of (in the British case) an imperial state and a ruling class. Today, however, what the incomers cannot help sensing is a potential for the opposite: failure, latent fragility and growing disorientation.

And added to this is a disconcerting lack of response (so far) from the majority. The English 80+ per cent – the 'by extension British', as Bikhu Parekh's *Report* describes them – remain cocooned in an inherited complacency, and the style of deprecation which used to suit the United Kingdom so well. They are unwilling to take 'little England' seriously. It may also be that the greatly aggravated public–private split I mentioned earlier plays a part here. A society suffering (as it were) from Basildon-style 'privatisation' can be little inclined to take identity questions seriously – whether Old-Brit or New-English.

But of course, this gives an opportunity for identitarian preachers to step in – frequently from the periphery. At least for a time, their rôle (and self-importance) stands to be enhanced by the disintegration in course around them. Salvationism may appeal to a Protestant sensibility more pronounced in Wales, Scotland and Ulster. The social DNA of that inheritance was previously the Kingdom of Heaven, thinly disguised as Great Britain. The disguise has to be heavier these days – but this can be read as meaning that even louder sermons are required. Such orations also sound better in a peripheral accent – if only because no one would now take them seriously, were they uttered in the old-fashioned ultra-English of 'Received Pronunciation'.

France does not suffer from the same problem. François Mitterrand may have made his jokes about 'little Corsica'(see below) but never had to bother about 'little France'. Politically speaking no such country was conceivable. Last-stage Britishness, on the other hand, is increasingly regulated by a need to stave off or neutralise *England*. The latter is a country not only conceivable, but now bearing down rapidly upon its inhabitants and knocking upon its own historical door, so to speak, in a way unlikely to be long denied. The door is damnably hard to open; but this also means people will knock louder, with mounting exasperation. When William Hague recently outlined his main ambition for the next Conservative government as being 'To return this country to its people!', he was ostensibly talking 'Britain' but almost certainly meaning England. The rhetoric remains statist and non-ethnic; but the denotation is of course angled towards an audience which (like Mr Ramonet in *Le Monde diplomatique* – see below) has never made much real distinction between 'British' and 'English' at all.

Such insouciance is sometimes seen as healthy, or as demonstrating a sturdy indifference to narrow or racial matters. However, it has a weakness inseparable from this great virtue: what was formerly 'British' could very easily *drift* into signifying Englishness, without demanding much or any conversion process on the way. No epiphany may be required along this particular Damascus Road: there is nowhere else it could end up. Under a New Conservative régime (for example) such an elision could come about via an added dose of Europhobia, with or even without some added resentment about Devolution, Scottish rapacity and Irish misconduct. The semantic barrier between 'English' and 'British' is low, slippery and traversable in both directions.

The context is already being prepared for a general switch of that sort, by the fevers of collapse and disappointment. This has been amusingly underlined by Anne McElvoy in a recent *Independent* column. She points out that the foot-and-mouth episode abruptly revealed how hysterically ambivalent the self-esteem of 'Britain' has already become. The British are either a Cool great power still cruising the *grand large*, or 'the worst, the most depressed and self-abasing country going: a blasted landscape of bestial epidemics, rail disasters, fuel crises and the over-long winter.' (*Independent*, 13 April 2001). She compares the Britannic roller-coaster with Russia (mercifully omitting Serbia from her frame of reference), as exhibiting how nervous post-imperial countries can become, as they teeter unstably between one stereotype and the next. Fate has decreed them either wondrous Great, or else Hell upon Earth – but never, well . . . 'ordinary'. What they seem to dread most is this intervening *terrain vague*. The latter is coming yet for all that (she concludes): 'Both pessimism without hope of redemption and bouncy optimism are . . . distortions of our real situation, which is that of a medium-sized country, trying to make the best of the hand history, geography, temperament and climate have dealt us. *Live with it*'.

No immigrant intellectual or politico from such born-ordinary sites as Scotland and Wales can fail to find all this familiar. The inferiority/superiority complex has been like mother's schizophrenia to most of them. Scotland and Wales have always been known as edgeland dumps peopled by half-humans unable to 'manage on their own'. Except (that is) when they were being the greatest wee countries upon earth, responsible for nearly all inventions (including the British Empire) and capable of occasionally trashing the 'old enemy', on or off the sports-ground. The cringe and the chest-beating went hand-in-hand. Sometimes one was encouraged to pretend this was an *interesting* way of life.

But it was also a mindset which depended on believing that *Britain was different*. The all-British identity once stood for durable escape from such dispiriting dilemmas of the native heath. Britishness in those days was like the stable broader platform upon which migrants could lead sane and upwardly-mobile lives, punctuated by occasional returns to a native terrain made roseate in retrospect. Thus distance lent more than enchantment to the eye – its accompaniment was a kind of self-indulgent weekend 'nationalism', the harmless vaunting of differences nobody took very seriously, and which in a way actually strengthened the appeal of the broader platform. But now they find the platform itself disintegrating beneath their feet. Their life-chances are being taken away from them, by selfish nationalists. As Ms McElvoy perceives so clearly, cringing-and-chest-thumping is spreading like foot-and-mouth. The English are ceasing to be so reliably British, hence 'greater' than themselves, hence able to encompass (and reward) others. Before long they might end up as themselves: post-imperial *English*.

This must be stopped. At all costs the precious 'dual identity' of Scot-Brits, Cymric- and Ulster-Brits has to be saved. The logic is plain. Preserving these hybrids will help preserve the heartland itself from fatal shrinkage: hence nationalism in the periphery must be arrested first, by a tighter policing of Devolution. That will avoid what has come to be called the 'backlash' – an unseemly and irritated reaction from the majority. The backlash is invariably imagined as a menace. It is derogation from duty – never just an adaptation to the times, a route to normalisation, or even progress. The Ukanian game-rules naturally inhibit such thoughts. The latter half-imply that Little England might turn out to be *better*, more democratic and generally more livable than the inherited Hulk of Providence, upon which sails All We Hold Dear. Which would imply in turn that, as Tim Garton Ash suspects, the Kingdom within which we languish United is finished, or – at the very least – due for rational replacement by constitutional reform.

Among peripheral Brit-missionaries, conviction on such matters tends towards the Jesuitical in its intensity. They are unshakably convinced that Little England would be by definition narrow, powerless, despised and probably 'Anglo-Saxon' in that caustic quasi-racial sense so dear to the French. More important, it might well turn against *them*, the missionaries. English voters preferring *not* to have a Scottish, Welsh or Ulster Premier (or Chancellor of the Exchequer) would be the end of the world. Best ban the thought from the drawing-room, therefore, until the Union can be sufficiently revived, and the world again made safe for weekend nationalism and folk-dancing. In the meantime, revivalism must be guaranteed by ever louder proclamations and stratagems of loyalty, by the selective vindication of British achievements, laced with snarling denunciations of 'separatism' and parochialism, plus (in New Labour's case) the brutish imposition of Party loyalism in the working-class ghettos.

More recent immigrants are placed in a real dilemma here. The result is often an inability to choose sides. That is, to decide between making the best of the hulk, or opting more frankly for a democratic replacement. Were the latter a popular movement, with mass support and any prospect of taking over the system, there would probably be no contest here. I quoted earlier from one of the most brilliant and prophetic accounts of Thatcherism's rise, Stuart Hall's 'Moving Right Show' of the late 1970s. Thirty years on, this analysis by a Caribbean-British sociologist remains crucial to all serious critiques of late Britain.

But the one-time Editor of *New Left Review* is now a contributor to a *Report* made necessary by the very same ongoing 'show' he was then denouncing – Blairism's prosecution of all the Thatcherite *motifs* within a mainly unreformed United Kingdom. The dilemma of the present day is constituted by the absence of any 'replacement', either socialist or democratic. This is why Lord Parekh's *Report* is compelled to vacillate. On one hand 'The word "British" will never do on its own'; yet on the other hand (actually lower down on the same page) – 'Britishness is not ideal, but at least it appears acceptable, particularly when suitably qualified – Black British, Indian British, British Muslim, and so on'.

In practice, 'acceptable', put-up-with-it 'Britain' then remains in command, and *Multi-Ethnic Britain* turns into another recommended range of changes for the hulk – still another informal 'constitution' for the UK. But this is only what everyone is forced to do in 'Britain'. Because the elective dictatorship precludes formal constitutional change, all dissidents end up proposing their own informal constitutions: blueprints of regionalism, multinational ground-plans, postmodern levitation schemes or (as here) suggestions for a more multicultural society and polity. These are not 'proposals' at all, but notions set hopefully afloat upon the Ukanian stream, in the belief that elements of the élite *must* remain 'open to ideas'. Via such apertures – by think-tank labyrinth, 'great debate', stern Editorial, patient committee-work or even the House of Lords – some deformed remnant may then one day figure as 'My government's *radical* modernisation plans'.

On the general theme of Old Corruption versus New Constitution, I have included an exchange between myself and Yasmin Alibhai-Brown of the *Independent* as an Appendix (see p. 163 below). This was written in 2000, well before the 2001 election. Unfortunately, all too little has changed between then and now. It seems to me that the June election simply aggravated the unacceptability of all-British Redemptionism, moving it towards outright reaction rather than the circumspect conservatism which could once have been counted upon. There is probably even less opportunity now for what Alibhai-Brown aspired to. In 2001 (for example) new restrictions were imposed on 'asylum-seekers', by which HM's Immigration Service was directed to be doubly suspicious of 'Kurds, Roma, Tamils, Pontic Greeks, Somalis and Afghans'. More rigorous examination was required of such cases than of 'other persons in the same circumstances'. As Hugo Young pointed out in the *Guardian* (8 May), most of these are from stateless populations with no passport. Where this is not the case, the issuing states (Afghanistan, Albania, Somalia) are unlikely to complain. Personal appearance and what detectives like to

call 'material evidence' will settle the matter, all the more easily since –
amazingly – 'it is not necessary to provide the information in a language
which the applicant understands'.

The 8th of May was a month before the vote, and a hysterical campaign
to prevent 'so-called asylum-seekers' from 'flooding in' was being conducted
by the Conservative Party. It was the moment to start looking tough, and
thus demonstrate – 'not only that Labour has become, in a vital area, as bad
as the Tories, but that it has lost its intellectual as well as its moral faculties'.
Corruption of this order relies on 'the building of a wall of righteous self-
belief . . . A power-driven certainty that, because one is who one is, one can
by definition do no wrong.' Or (as I think one might also say) 'Britishness'
by any other name doth smell as foul – above all when engaged upon winning an election, while simultaneously proclaiming its anti-racism.

'England and therefore by extension Britain . . .' the *Report* says. But the
logical corollary of that is: 'Britain and therefore *by contraction*
England . . .', where the rate of lessening is pretty small, and in fact denotes
a scatter of widely divergent (and often ambiguous) populations stretching from St Helier to Derry/Londonderry and out to Lerwick. Recent
incomers are predominantly concentrated in England, and it is not obvious why they (any more than the natives) should be over-anxious about
the distinction. It would be different if English identity was overdeveloped
like (say) Great Serb nationalism. But of course the specific dilemma here
is the contrary: an English nationalism remarkably 'backward' in the sense
of being both stretched and divided between the poles of 'Britishness' and
a somehow abbreviated and intolerable 'Little England'.

Proponents of reluctant 'acceptability' often point how *relatively* good
the story of race relations has been in the United Kingdom, when compared to other European countries or the United States. This observation
is correct, but usually averts its gaze from what is by far the most likely
explanation: the remarkably low salience of host-community *ethnicity*, in

the sense of 'Englishness'. Almost unformulated *politically*, this has been an atmospheric rather than an ideological phenomenon. Racist movements since the 1930s have invariably presented themselves as loudly and offensively 'British', even while exploiting the most local resentments of mono-ethnic communities. 'Britishness' in this sense of course automatically transports the imagination on to a grander plane of aspiration, gilding festering local grudges with fantasies of blood-descent and endemic superiority. Here, 'English' denotes only the local chapter of a mythological clan (or Klan) – no longer that loose mixture of earlier immigrants who were half-united as '*Angleterre*', before suffering conquest by the Norman-French.

This historical style of vagueness may permit 'acceptability', as the authors of *Multi-Ethnic Britain* hope. But it can do so only at the cost of perpetuating the rest of Britishness as well – with all the injustices and pitfalls which Parekh's *Report* so eloquently denounces. 'Identities' hang together and reproduce a structure of authority, in this case the miserable half-elected 'dictatorship' of a United Kingdom on the skids. Putting up with it for fear of something worse can also mean preventing something better from having a chance. Would there be risks in constitutional reform where English (or English-regional) identity takes political shape? Perhaps – but would they really be worse than those of helping to conserve such an ambiguous and faltering hegemony?

The success of incomers has always depended upon a certain rate of change, and innovation: positive development, inside which differences of background and culture come to appear secondary, unimportant or forgiveable. Is this not as true of constitutional change as of the socio-economic sort? A political world of unfolding possibilities and opportunities is surely more fertile terrain than the rather grudging 'acceptability' of the Westminster *status quo* preached by *The Future of Multi-Ethnic Britain*.

There is still another twist to this argument which surfaces little in the *Report*. While it deals with the statutory categories of statehood and internal identity, like 'Britain', 'Wales' and so on, an extraordinary amount of the actual content of new-immigration has very little rapport with these. Most immigration has been not just to England, but to the one zone of that historic territory which has grown away from it both economically and sociologically: London. According to the Institute of Race Relations (IRR) database, black people make up 6.2 per cent of the English population, but over 25 per cent of Londoners. And the large number of non-black incomers only underlines how heterogeneous the capital of both England and Great Britain has become: in current terminology, a vast 'multicultural' (or even 'cosmopolitan') metropolis doubling up as the institutional centre of a nation-state. The 'greater' capital is (as mentioned above) also ever less distinguishable from the region about it: 'Roseland' or the geographical South-East.

In an overview of 'The Fall of Great Powers', historian William McNeill argues that what he calls 'the civilized norm of laminated polyethnicism' is re-establishing itself in the contemporary world. Urbanisation has exhausted its former sources in industrial-revolution homelands such as the British–Irish archipelago, North America and Western Europe. Hence continued expansion pulls in migrants from further afield – from other continents and the former 'Third World'. Japan alone has refused this tendency. 'Interaction and mutual adjustment is certain' (he goes on), '. . . but assimilation of these newcomers into a single, seamless citizen body, as called for by democratic theory, is highly improbable in the foreseeable future.'[44]

---

44 William McNeill, 'The Fall of Great Powers', in *The Review*, vol. XVII, spring 1994, pp. 123–43.

Far from deploring this problem, McNeill welcomes it as a return of 'the Eurasian style of old-fashioned polyethnicity' that flourished before the age of modern nationalism. However, he concedes that it will take a long time to resolve. It is likely to be 'the most critical question of the next century for rich nations confronting incipient demographic decay and substantial immigration of physically distinct, religiously different, and (to begin with) desperately poor outsiders'. In the circumstances of British disintegration, the question is especially critical. This is mainly because the 'rich nation' facing most of the challenge, England, finds itself gravely handicapped by constitutional sclerosis. The general deficits of Western 'democratic theory' are bad enough. In the UK, these are tied to deficits of practice and incomprehension, which appear likely to expose it to strenuous 'interaction and mutual adjustment' for (at least) a long time to come. Here, the interaction has become inseparable from the conflicts of Devolution and Northern Ireland, and from the British state's quandary over Europe.

The results of the 2001 census will not be known for some time yet. But they are very likely to show a metropolis in which the IRR's old figure of 25 per cent black population has been left well behind – that is, a polyethnic Greater London in even stronger contrast with the rest of England. Over the 2001 election period it was noticeable how inter-racial violence marked smaller towns in the North and the Midlands, rather than London. As in Ulster, the 'border areas' generate most conflicts: the zones where resentful natives turn on invaders, and the latter respond by asserting their rights. But in the English case these communities are now uncomfortably like McNeill's – London polyethnicity on one side, and an abandoned or retreating countryside on the other. Two Englands, therefore: New Labour's 'Roseland', versus an England not merely 'little' but marginalised, where the defeated turn to the political Right, like Duncan Smith's Conservatism or even Nicholas Griffin's British National Party. This developing antithesis will make it even harder than before for 'England' to re-frame itself as a single political entity. All English regionalism has to face the dilemma of one overwhelming region, the 'Great Wen' of tradition now swollen to irreversible centrality as a multicultural city-state eclipsing all others.

10   LAST-GASP BRITONS

Intellectuals want to be the fleas on the top dog.
Ferdinand Mount, *The National Interest* (May 2001)

In a talk I gave in 2000, called 'Farewell Britannia', I argued that the fixed idea of Britain 'breaking up' neatly into the classical four ethnicities (England, Scotland, Ireland, Wales) was both unlikely and undesirable.[45] Break-up was no longer a theory but a fact; however, this 'fact' was increasingly untidy, and should be acknowledged as such. Could not replacement of the anachronistic constitution and its residually imperial traditions be accomplished in other ways? Indeed (I incautiously suggested) had not an alternative perspective already been adumbrated – the British-Irish Council, or 'Council of the Isles'?

This originated as one part ('Strand Three') of the 1998 Peace Agreement in Northern Ireland, in an attempt to reassure Protestant opinion that institutional links would be kept even with a devolved United Kingdom. But other brands of opinion at once welcomed the plan with enthusiasm. There were emerging constituencies of opinion all too ready to welcome any way out from the dead cul-de-sac of Britishness. The Dublin government supported it materially, nationalist spokesmen in Wales and Scotland saw it as an additional platform for airing their views,

45 See *New Left Review*, New Series, No. 7 (Jan.–Feb. 2001), 'Farewell Britannia', pp. 55–74.

the island Dependencies valued it as an unusual form of recognition, and Regionalists within England hoped that in time they also might find a place there. However tentative and uncertain, the proposal dispelled some of the claustrophobia from 'Britain' by merely evoking a changing archipelago. It was felt to be dispelling part of the unitarist miasma which had since 1979 settled upon the retreating Westminster state. Surely, greater variety and emergent equality must lie somewhere in such a script?

This is why (I must now concede) it will never get anywhere. The watchdogs will never allow it. A polity on the skids may throw off such intimations of its own demise. But it does so in order to postpone and mislead. The 'British-Irish Council' was in truth the Un-British-and-Irish Council of the Isles, intended to foster an auriole of hope and credulous aspiration among those taking it seriously. It was another part of the Redemption variety show – an audience-befuddler, prompting reveries of life after Unionism. But the point of the dreams was to keep Unionism alive, not to transcend it. As opposed to the tacit non-thought so prized by Edmund Burke, 'thinking' has now been compelled to evolve into the public or state arena. But in what is still Burke's Britain, it can evolve only as another survival technique. 'Thoughts' are in this context incapable of realisation. Though advertised as brilliant new swimming strokes, they are in truth ways of treading water.

Effective implementation of the British-Irish Council's pseudo-scheme always implied some more defined rôle for England (or English regions) distinct from the Union government at Westminster. Otherwise most representatives on it would have been in the ludicrous position of representing themselves directly *and* the central state indirectly, since none of them except the Irish Republic are independent. But Westminster would of course have to be directly present *as well*. On any politically important matter, the British-Irish Council would therefore have amounted to a classical form of idiocy: Ukania communing with Herself, via the assorted parts of Herself, occasionally punctuated by bits of negotiation with Dublin (which could quite well have been carried out anywhere else).

This tragic–comic absurdity was impressed more strongly on me by some remarks from Professor Paul Bew of Queen's University, Belfast, about 'Farewell Britannia'.[46] Like any serious Unionist, Professor Bew despised the British-Irish Council. The Belfast Agreement might be destroyed by Protestant opposition, war might be resumed, and bring a Protestant exodus over to Scotland, England and Wales. Many have half-foreseen such an emergency in the past, like Conor Cruise O'Brien. In the conclusion of his *Memoir* (1998) he argues that the Ulster Protestants may in the end be compelled into a deal with 'constitutional nationalism', if the British Union deserts them. They might then be well advised to seek 'inclusion in a united Ireland', under conditions guaranteeing their minority rights and status. However, there is a second possibility – emigration to Scotland. He elaborates farther:

> Paradoxically, the flight option is made psychologically more attractive as the prospect of Scottish independence grows, and antipathy to what is seen as English betrayal grows . . . Almost subliminally, the Scottish option has been creeping up upon the unionist middle classes. Scottish universities have been flooded for years with students from Northern Ireland as increasing numbers find a triumphalist republican ethos in Ulster's two universities unacceptable . . .

Such immigrants would mostly vote Unionist (Tory or Labour) and presumably go on disliking Catholics as much as they had done in Ulster. In 'Farewell Britannia', all I pointed out was that this might be less than welcome in a *democratic* Scotland moving towards independence, where an

---

46 *Times Literary Supplement*, 16 March 2001.

SNP-led government could be in power on (obviously) anti-Unionist grounds. Such a state would also have to try and transcend the sectarian feuds which until recently disfigured the West of Scotland. The very last thing it would welcome is an injection of embittered *pied-noir* politics from across the Irish Sea.

'This is a remarkable passage', objected Bew, '[c]an anyone imagine a similar tone being employed in a Left/liberal magazine towards any other group in British society?' In other words, are Ulstermen now to be treated as *worse than blacks*? He interprets the angry tone of 'Farewell Britannia' as arising from 'an embrace of ethnic nationalism, which is surely one of the more surprising side effects of the collapse of the original New Left Project'.

There is no such embrace, either in the text aimed at by Bew or (as far as I know) in anything ever published by *New Left Review*, past or present, collapsed or regenerated. Any irate tone in the 'Farewell Britannia' essay came from sheer despair over the spectacle of a Unionism determined to hold everybody else in the archipelago back upon its own level of archaic, limpet-like Britishness. Naturally no such Unionist can perceive anything but 'ethnic nationalism' in *any* political opposition to 'Britain'. But this because the Union is still perceived as having been (and in some vestigial way as still being) the Chosen People: that is, the bearers of *all* civic-democratic nationality against ethnic heathens. Since it is the Chosen who incarnate Reason, outwith their embrace lies nothing but backsliding and atavism.

The context of Professor Bew's critique was an article extolling, of all things, the perennial wisdom of *Edmund Burke*. In the year 2001, this was surely far more remarkable than any observations made in my article about current changes. For the authentic Burkean, nothing can ever change – save of course in the 'evolutionary' manner of blueprinted Britishness. Patrician or Lampedusan adjustment, that is, calculated to leave the essence ever more firmly and unchangeably itself. The 'profoundly Burkean original vision' that Bew would like to see rejuvenated was in truth a concoction of commercialism and aristocracy which suited the period it came from. But today it is a coelacanth, alive only because of its lingering convenience to the City of London, rather than to the citizens of the United Kingdom. Thomas Paine pointed out at the time how it bestowed sumptuous imaginary vestments upon forms of hard-eyed corruption and rapacity: those very forms from which, two centuries later, the archipelago is still trying to escape (and Blairism is struggling in vain to 'modernise'). Burkeism consecrated a national and imperial victory over the French, and of course helped to build up the long expansive era of the United Kingdom state-nation. But to imagine that this same formula may rescue the latter from today's disintegration is itself a sort of madness.

In her recent study of Orangeism, Ruth Dudley Edwards called the Ulster Unionists *The Faithful Tribe* – devotees of the undying Union which once stood not just for Protestant doctrines but for freedom and progress against superstition, poverty and barbarism. Such faith has of course also been a bizarre version of 'self-determination': a political will for merger, or coalescence, rather than for a separate nation-state. However, this wish plainly depends *entirely* on the host-state's agreement and integrity. In Bob Purdie's phrase, Ulster subjects are 'tenants-at-will' of the Crown, not members by Treaty (like the Scots and the Dependencies), or even by conquest and assimilation (like the Welsh).[47] On the host side the 'agreement'

---

47 In the *Weekly Guardian* of 23–29 August 2001, Jonathan Freedland reported on a new opinion survey which showed that 41 per cent of respondents believe Northern Ireland should be united with the Republic, while *only 26 per cent thought it should stay part of the UK*. This seems to be founded on general impatience with a never-ending problem: when asked whom they blamed, few respondents blamed either the IRA or the Unionist ultras separately, but 64 per cent said 'both sides are equally responsible'. Obviously a UK popular vote would on these figures result in withdrawal – which means ultra-Protestantism is even more completely dependent upon the Union *state* than had been thought.

part may have been unimportant under the old Burkean conditions, where a supranational élite decided 'on behalf of' the various populations. Everywhere outside Queen's University, we live in post-Burkean times. In the decrepitude of the United Kingdom, however, we have not yet fully arrived in *constitutional* times either. Tom Paine's day has still not arrived.

Ulster Unionism has become a conspiracy to hold that day forever in abeyance. It was greatly fortified by the 2001 June election. In Northern Ireland an electoral campaign unrecognisably different from that elsewhere in the UK (with no signs of apathy or poor turnout) produced a sharply polarised country. West of the Bann *Sinn Féin* achieved its most impressive poll victory, displacing the Social Democratic Labour Party as main representative of Ulster's Catholics. East of the Bann an analogous triumph by the Democratic Unionist Party (or Paisleyites) suggested that a majority of Protestants may now have become hostile to the Northern Ireland Assembly. Three weeks later, Unionist leader David Trimble resigned as First Minister of the Assembly, and the whole Belfast Agreement fell under threat (from which it was rescued only by great ingenuity in the winter of 2001–2002). After the 7th of June, paramilitary activity looked certain to increase, and lead to a resumption of direct rule from Westminster. This was avoided; but as long as the UK's Unwritten Constitution continues in business, it cannot be ruled out.

In the circumstances of post-2001 Blairism, it is not inconceivable that Protestant extremism could then turn into the vanguard of a general reaction with compatible aims. After all, Ulster Unionism mainly wants the customary ethos of Britishness to stay in place: Hogwarts-on-Thames, Black Rod, first-past-the-post, Charles the Third – whatever is needed to maintain the Kingdom's last-resort Sovereignty over Northern Ireland, for their own convenience. It depends upon maintaining the non-written Constitution, and on its continued insulation from democracy. It depends upon the mythology of the 'British Race' being strengthened, rather than challenged by reform or federalism. Ever since a Conservative government renounced 'strategic and economic interest' in maintaining British rule over Ulster, political *noblesse oblige* alone has remained.

In truth, that *noblesse* has dwindled away, at approximately the same rate as the popularity of the Windsor Monarchy. On the other side, the obligation to support democratic government in Northern Ireland is (fortunately) shared with the Irish Republic. 'Direct rule' continues as a possibility in Britain through constitutional inertia alone – that same unwillingness to undertake central reform which has consistently betrayed all late-British régimes since the 1960s. No democratic mandate to continue ruling Northern Ireland could ever be obtained, and no constitutional 'entrenchment' is possible for the same reasons as apply to Scotland and Wales. As R.W. Johnson says, there is simply no central written constitution to make it work, or to allot and enforce responsibilities. This is, surely, the most miserable of substitutes for Burkean tradition?

Yet Bew rules out any alternative. He even urges Blair to heed the example of the earlier William Gladstone rather than the late – that is, the pre-Home Rule Gladstone who still thought of Ireland as a 'constituent part of the United Kingdom', and sought to foster the 'one people' conception of Britain. This is indeed the fundamental dilemma of Unionism. There never has been one *people* to sustain the grand apparatus of Britishness and Empire. There was one *state*, and, crucially, one transnational *class* (Edmund Burke's patrons, originally). But these were incapable of forging one nation – and indeed, for most of the three-century span following 1688, they saw no need to do so. The Constitution Burke extolled was configured by *not* attempting to do so. So why should anyone expect it to suddenly switch tracks today, and embark upon a French-style politics of assimilation, through (as Bew puts it) 'the activist sponsorship of the central British state'?

This goes far beyond rewinding history. It is more like a wilful insanity of retrospect. I mentioned 'madness' already, which may appear rather harsh in relation to the desperate but sober views of Bew, Trimble and other Unionists. However, only a hair's breadth away from their position, there *are* voices clearly straight out of the asylum – the *Daily Mail*, for instance, bugle of 'Middle England' and reputed touchstone of some New Labour policy-makers. Regrettably, they are saying much the same thing as the Belfast Professors, but a good deal more raucously. Following a defence by former Foreign Secretary Cook of Devolution and multiculturalism on 19 April 2001, its front page screamed:

> ASTONISHING DECLARATION: THERE IS NO SUCH RACE AS THE BRITISH . . . Robin Cook caused a major political row last night after declaring that the British are not a race . . .

The theme is taken up on the inside pages by Tory philosopher Roger Scruton, who locates the source of racial Britishness in 'a long process of melding, in which at least three races – English, Welsh and Scots – have acquired common institutions, common customs, a common language and a common religion'.[48] From 'melding' there has emerged a super-race,

---

48 'Melding' is a card-players' term, given in the *Shorter Oxford Dictionary* as 'declaring' or announcing one's hand. *Webster's* more elaborate definition is: 'announcing a combination of cards with scoring value by placing them face up on the table'. Is the history of the Union therefore an interminable game of cards, in which races got shuffled, only to reappear again when the right (or wrong) combination is dealt out by Providence? This can hardly be what Professor Scruton was thinking of. But if he just meant 'mixing up', or some kind of blending, then surely the criteria divulged in his list of traits ('fair play', 'countryside', etc.) are simply preposterous. Is 'fair play' unknown in the Netherlands? Is *Italia Nostra*'s love of the countryside less than that of English Heritage? Is British advocacy of 'law rather than force' stronger than the American brand? Judging by this, 'melding' looks like a card-trick designed to make the card of *England* vanish.

therefore, defined by 'belief in liberty, democratic spirit, love of fair play and genius for compromise, attachment to the countryside and tolerance of . . . those who accept its customs and laws'. It must be galling for Ulster Unionists to see themselves so glibly omitted from Middle England's roll-call of the tribes. But what do they expect? They wanted to be taken for granted as loyal foot-soldiers of 'melding'; and they are.

A simpler explanation is that when many English intellectuals and politicos are forced to think about 'Britain' and England together, they *do* go 'mad'. This is not because they are those 'whom the gods wish to destroy', as Enoch Powell once darkly hinted. Rather, it is as if the 'one people/race' dilemma triggers the equivalent of a fit, or spasm, from which they find themselves momentarily unable to escape. The low semantic barrier between 'British' (dead but Great) and 'English' (desirable yet intolerable) sets up something like a computer loop. A form of Automatic Writing then takes over. Normal debates degenerate into séances, during which ancestral spirit-guides appear and fight it out in the respective craniums, relaying encrypted messages alternately from *Beowulf* (or J.R.R. Tolkien), Edmund Burke and the speeches of Churchill. These are usually mixed up with protestations of anti-racism, outreach affidavits and platitudinous conclusions like Scruton's.

Studying these, one can see that for the subjects 'England' and 'Britain' have become like Siamese twins. There can be no question of sacrificing one to save the other. What the Union of Britannic watchdogs demands is that *at all costs* both must be kept alive. William Empson partly diagnosed the condition a long time ago in *Seven Types of Ambiguity* (1949). In what he labelled as 'second-type' ambiguities, 'two or more alternative meanings are fully resolved into one' – but *which* one can depend upon the circumstances of the moment. This depends upon the poetical effect required. National narratives require such moments of lyricism. When the identity-narrative is summoned up, varying situations demand that the 'imagined community' be presented or re-presented in variable ways – to answer attacks or suggestions which are themselves shifting in implication.

Now and then the 'England' sibling must be resorted to: when peripheral nationalities are felt as obtrusive or demanding, for instance. In that case, 'What about us?', or '. . . the rest of us', can seem momentarily fitting. The brute fact of Englishness is unveiled. But unfortunately, all too little is revealed by the twitching curtain. At best it leads to the production of *lists*, in the style most famously associated with George Orwell's *The Lion and the Unicorn* (1940).[49] When the *meaning* of the data-string is questioned, however, the 'Britain' twin at once reassumes his rights: a spectral ancestor of the multinational *state* turns out to be England's mission, and her promise for the future – Liberty, Law, Decency and the Countryside, evoking what is in effect a stereotype of the patriciate's realm between 1746 and 1832.

The ambiguity thus resolved has a deeply conservative poetic message: 'Hang on to this jewel of time – and all may yet be well!' But the solution

---

49 *The Lion and the Unicorn* (1941):

> The clatter of clogs in the Lancashire mill towns, the to-and-fro of the lorries on the Great North Road, the queues outside the Labour Exchanges, the rattle of pin-tables in the Soho pubs, the old maids biking to Holy Communion through the mists of the autumn morning – all these are not only fragments, but *characteristic* fragments, of the English scene. How can one make a pattern out of this muddle? . . . Yes, there *is* something distinctive and recognizable in English civilization. It is a culture as individual as that of Spain. It is somehow bound up with solid breakfasts and gloomy Sundays, smoky towns and winding roads, green fields and red pillar-boxes. It has a flavour of its own. Moreover it is continuous, it stretches into the future and the past, there is something in it that persists, as in a living creature.

It is worth noting how Orwell's list had a discovering, interrogative note to it. This has vanished in the innumerable abusive stereotypes that have followed – citations looking back to the original as itself an embodiment of English ethnicity.

itself hides farther ambiguities. What is directly evoked is the 'Old England' of Christmas cards: squirely Georgian or Regency cavortings, that country for which elegies are today composed. The nostalgia touched here is deep, and visibly anachronistic – which is of course just what utilitarian or nationalist critics are complaining about. So what *is* being hung on to, and why can it be projected onward so confidently? The answer, unfortunately, is the City – the urban dimension of England-Britain, affirmed in global terms during the same Christmas-card epoch, and still a third-rate con-testant in post-1989's 'globalisation'. As described above by Ingham, Rubinstein and others, 'England' in modern times has largely meant 'London', and over the 1979–2001 period this centre of gravity has greatly multiplied its centrifugal power. Under Thatcher, Major and Blair, enhanced centralism has only echoed its magnetic expansion.

The effect upon the England/Britain twins is enormous. The expanding multinational domain of the patriciate did rest on a kind of balance between rural and urban. London was dominant, but not overwhelming. Since the 1960s, however, with the collapse of Northern manufacturing and the re-mobilisation of the City, the South-East has indeed become over-whelming – yet without intelligible forms of political dominance. The system does not permit these. It keeps going on contempt for central con-stitutional change and regionalism, so that 'Roseland' has in a functional sense *become* 'England', but completely *sans cérémonie*, more or less the way dry rot takes over a mansion. Within *this* state-nation, a territorial nation-ality has been not so much marginalised as abandoned. The contrary of Roseland's 'mobilisation' is the rest of England's 'demobilisation': it has been left to its own devices, as it were, with occasional grudging handouts from the Centre. Voiceless and grumbling, the North now furnishes a swelling tide of emigrants to 'Roseland' and a reliable body of 'cannon-fodder' (compliant back-bench MPs) to the Westminster party in office. Obviously, an 'England' that merely took over the Centre from its Siamese sibling, 'Britain', would mean extremely little. As anyone in Tyne and Wear or Cornwall can see, it might even spell *more* 'London domination'.

This is the real background to the hopelessness of the England–Britain 'debate'. It also helps explain why 'Britain' always gets the somewhat crazed upper hand in all such arguments. No other rhetorical solution is available – and *this* exit also happens to suit and support the existing state and authority-structure. Preservation of an archaic Crown and Constitution is not so much the best, as the *only available* way of maintaining secure forward motion. Constitutional reform, by contrast, would usher in a host of unknowns.

What is entirely unassailable on democratic grounds – as the Jenkins Commission laid them out – remains potentially troublesome on *national* grounds. The England which, in the famous over-quoted phrase, 'has not spoken yet' was in truth prevented from speaking, by the suffocating and combined identities of Toryism *and* 'British Socialism'. Such absence of voice is then diagnosed as a kind of witless ethnicity. If they have not spoken for so long, it can only be because they have something perfectly frightful to say – a message 'Anglo-Saxon' or worse. The tongue-tied dilemma is rarely a matter of hypocrisy or deceit. The speaker almost invariably *believes* the message imparted at a given instant – on this subject, indeed, he or she believes it passionately and with personal commitment.

With similar shrewdness, Empson points out in the 'Introduction' to his collection *Argufying*: 'Roughly . . . the moral is that a developing society decides practical questions more by the way it interprets words it thinks obvious and traditional than by its official statements of current dogma'.[50]

---

50 *Argufying* (Chatto and Windus 1987) p. 7. Empson's editor John Haffenden suggests that Empson's Introduction to these essays was 'summing up his first three books', including *Seven Types of Ambiguity*.

In other words, Blairism is now better defined by how it 'stands up for Britain' than by the tenebrous incantations of the Third Way. Here the practical question being resolved by an oscillation between twinned meanings is that 'Britain' remains absolutely necessary. 'England' is of course unavoidable – indeed, ever less avoidable after Devolution, if only from the constraints of the 'West Lothian Question'. It existed as an historic state long before 1688, or even 1066, and today over 80 per cent of the population under the 'British' umbrella would accept the label (and not only at football Internationals or cricket Test Matches). But its *important* emotive meaning remains 'Britain': not Anglo-Saxon inheritance, freckles, warmish beer (and so on) but 'liberty', 'fair play', 'tolerance' (and so forth). These recycled clichés of Whig history still, in fact, carry an echo of lump-in-the-throat Greatness. What the interpretation voices is this traditional, 'obvious' poetry, a narrative of aspiration which (for all the mounting contrary evidence) has to be fallen back upon whenever challenged.

Such battles are conceptually inconclusive, of course. But peripheral watchdogs and the *Daily Telegraph* (as well as the *Mail*) applaud the resultant ravings. So does the British National Party, from the zones of deprivation in which the dregs of racism survive – invariably flagged as British, not 'English'. And at least the New House of Lords is still standing, ready to welcome all those who rave of England. A tumbledown Music Hall rather than a modern Senate; but still our own, and still with that touch of Greatness about it. When in 1955 Nigel Dennis published his prophetic joke on the old régime, *Cards of Identity*, he could not have imagined by how immensely far the reality of a tatterdemalion state would one day leave behind the keenest satire of that age.

11 FOLIES DE GRANDEUR

Sovereignty must not be the last word in our history . . . Our place in the world and our influence upon it now depend upon accepting a plural, diversified France. Only this pluralism and a determined break with National-Republican ideology (now largely a matter of rhetoric) will give us a viable role inside a European Union, itself much more pluralist as it extends its membership.

Jean-Marie Colombani, *Les infortunes de la République* (Grasset 2000), pp. 154 and 174

I mentioned earlier the mounting tide of condemnations of the UK from abroad. In the April 2001 number of *Le Monde diplomatique*, another such grave verdict was delivered by its Editor upon the matter of Britain: '*Angleterre, crise totale*'. Mr Ramonet observes rightly enough that the current 'plague' manifests something wrong with the country in which it is occurring: a 'latent cruelty' and previously hidden 'perversions of the spirit' among politicians and people alike. He goes on to list the now familiar symptoms: disasters, another winter of even profounder discontent, the palpable failure of privatisations, spiteful Europhobia and intolerance of the foreign and intrusive, redoubled servitude towards the USA.

No one can contest his diary of pestilence and futility. When he turns to explain the pattern, however, an undue simplicity is at once in evidence. We find that slavish 'neo-liberalism' is alone held responsible. Hence Blair and the New-Labourites have 'changed nothing'. Their variant of Thatcher's (or Reagan's) gospel has merely extended its appalling consequences, increased the rich–poor divide, lowered the public sector's share in GDP, let medical care slide towards the bottom of the European league (and so on). It is time the European Left drew much sterner conclusions from this tableau, by treating the heirs of 'British Socialism' as pariahs too. Instead of which (he concludes bitterly) the Euro-Socialists looked quite likely to elect Robin Cook as their President at a forthcoming conference in Berlin (this failed to happen).

Marketolatry and Clintonesque servility have indeed marked, and disfigured, both the body and the soul of *Angleterre* (meaning 'Britain'). They have been necessary conditions of New Labour rule. Without some internalisation of neo-liberal superstitions, Blairism could not have built up its present hegemony. However, it is inaccurate to blame these things so completely for the country's present fate. Mr Ramonet fails to acknowledge the substantial (if often hypocritical) part played by anti-marketism in the Third Way rhetoric itself, and also in Chancellor Brown's economic stewardship. Crooks are undoubtedly at work, but they are not (or don't start up as) mere *vendus*. No selling of souls has taken place, either at the outset or later. It may be more accurate to say that those responsible have edged sideways into ignominy, under a range of pressures which this style of critique largely fails to recognise. The typical disposition of Mr Ramonet's great newspaper is to assume that most sin emanates from failure (possibly wilful) to acknowledge the set of transnational abstract verities so infallibly broadcast by *Le Monde diplomatique*.

In reality, the contemporary fall of Britishness has derived from a quite positive *national* project – that inherited set of still inescapable 'dominant traditions' or structures, in Tocqueville's sense, which were simply rehatched in Blair's self-conscious 'Project' of 1997 and 2001. However deplorable, the latter is in a deeper sense not so different from those which have marked the Fifth Republic. Ignoring national destiny in a critique of another nation can be a way of ignoring the same thing in one's own.

Uneven development has produced a variation of tempo, naturally. In their middle period (the nineteenth and early twentieth centuries) the British state-nation was much stronger than its cousin over the Channel. Today the opposite is true. François Mitterrand (for instance) felt that in his own lifetime the balance had been reversed: the shame of 1940 had been replaced by the great 'second revolution' of the Fifth Republic, and notably by his own Presidency. However, this should not blind us to the deeper resemblance: post-Cold War France and Britain are both grappling with forms of state-nation redemption, in a shifting European context which is less and less favourable to them. Both remain founded on eighteenth-century templates. And both are attempting to stave off what they apprehend as the death-throes of downsizing and dependency.

Unlike De Gaulle's régime, the UK's statist identity made the mistake of rushing into neo-liberal affiliation from 1979 forwards, and now finds it hard (maybe impossible) to right the balance. But that impetus itself arose out of the reproductive necessities of a failing state, rather than from Free-Tradery as such, or from an intellectual resistance to corporate Europeanism. It was more than a refusal of 'L'Europe-puissance', whether in President Chirac's vision, or in the loftily left-of-centre configuration preferred by Pierre Bourdieu and Le Monde diplomatique. Refusal to acknowledge the UK's specific dilemma is a way of ignoring an equivalently specific contradiction in France.

In After Britain (Granta Books 1998) I made a satirical comparison between the UK and the last phase of the Hapsburg Empire in Central Europe. Alas, crueller and more recent analogies are also possible. Realms of lookalike impersonation have appeared in the wake of the Soviet Union and the Yugoslav Republic as well. When these undemocratic polities ceased being sustainable, they also have been characterised by chest-beating rhetoric (military or political, or both, but invariably strident). There also intense think-tank activity and piecemeal 'reforms' were undertaken to prop up the greatness of Russia and Serbia. Whatever the majority of Russians and Serbs thought, their ruling strata found the relinquishment of grandeur intolerable. They felt that they ('the Nation') simply could not go on existing without a standing-tall, effective identity in the world, and an accompanying '*rayonnement*' (somehow the French term is best, no doubt because the concept was patented there).

This patent-makers' view of Redemption has recently been expounded in a slim volume called *Les cartes de la France à l'heure de la mondialisation*, by French Foreign Minister Hubert Védrine (Fayard 2000). The hand which France still has to play in globalisation times turns out to be weirdly similar to Blair's. Paris also retains world-power delusions and vanity, and thinks itself entitled to a 'special capacity' for intervention or pressure. Sometimes this is assisted by membership of European Union. Yes, Europe can be quite useful to grandeur. Far from dying off, in the post-Cold War climate such exceptionalism may actually be reviving.

This is a chilling thought. We find it expressed here more clearly than in the orations of Blair, or those of his former Foreign Secretary, Robin Cook. The latter did invent a supposedly ethical foreign policy, but with a less pseudo-philosophical framework. However, an evident parallelism persists in practice: that of ex-imperial states attempting not just to keep the accumulated assets, but in small ways to regain their former leverage and (the favoured UK expression) their 'clout'. If I place some emphasis on comparison here, it is partly to avoid any suggestion of an over-familiar response to denigration of the British state: 'being like the French'. Partly, this is because there has never been the smallest chance of the UK emulating a French modernisation model, or of British nationalism becoming more French in style. But also (more importantly), because upon another level, these states are so exactly like one another. Both are still managed by 'gangs' in the sense used before – élites formed in quite different ways, but both from another age and equivalently alien from the emergent new Europe.

The unkind way to put Védrine's theory is to say that the disintegration of the 'hyper-powers' (the USSR and American-led NATO) leaves increasing room for such manoeuvres by these post-imperial recidivists. The great thaw in the world is liberating not just small-timers like Ireland or Norway, but the former state-nation gang-bosses as well. The latter are down on their luck, but by no means out of business. They still have nuclear arms – the 'ultimate coinage of modern state power' as Michael Ignatieff has put it – Security Council standing, and powerful busybody instincts.[51] Such resurrected mobsters cannot help feeling they may now be in a position to pull a bit more rank over the ordinary and despicable.

The latter include most existing members of the United Nations, who in the Védrine optic turn out to be either 'mere states' or 'pseudo-states': totally lacking in clout and culture, in fact – the majority of them with scarcely a shred of grandeur to their names. In addition, they are all too inclined to go for English as their *lingua franca*. The Scandinavians are particularly culpable here: far too concerned with social justice and equality, and not nearly interested enough in '*l'Europe-puissance*'.

This resurrection of the London and Paris *mafiosi* could be especially dangerous for European Union, as last year's Nice conference and treaty made clear. A new *entente cordiale* against ordinariness might be the condition of fuller UK participation, and (as both the 2000 Danish vote against the Euro and Ireland's recent rejection of the Nice Treaty have shown) this might lead to mounting disaffection among the continent's many prosperous nonentities and 'mere states', mainly in the North and East. These are no-chancers who think that democracy is more significant than clout. In any great-power perspective (however decayed), that stands of course for cemetery road. The UK's Leader claims to foresee a Decision

---

51 'Bush's First Strike', *New York Review of Books*, 29 March 2001.

coming on the matter of the Euro-currency some time after his renewed 2001 mandate, but it may not happen. Solidarity among state-nations is notoriously difficult of attainment, and these are (after all) élites which have heartily detested one another for centuries.

One penalty of 'globalisation' seems to be that each state generates its own take upon the universal blessing/curse. Great-nationalist optics are not so easily discarded, and normally cross any Left–Right spectrum. There are substantial sectors of both British and French opinion which remain quite unable to perceive either Europe or the world except through their own post-imperial spectacles. The French pair has been restored a lot better than its Anglo-Brit equivalent, and gives much clearer focus and political coherence. This is why there is a French Left, as well as a Right, still capable of imagining only a centralised, major-power Europe built out of what Védrine calls the 'genetic code' of Frenchness – political as well as linguistic, anti-American, social-democratic and 'republican' in an unmistakably Gallic sense. This is the view from which (in the text quoted above) Jean-Marie Colombani says the French must at all costs liberate themselves. It stands for the equivalent of British 'Sovereignty', unitarism and 'elective dictatorship'.

This is the kind of conclusion Norman Davies suggested in the conclusion to his encyclopaedic work *The Isles* (1999), a book which no true Unionist can stand. But it also suggests that the 'break-up' of the United Kingdom state may turn out to be part of a far wider European trend – 'the most positive aspect of the EU', as Davies puts it. I believe he is right. And it will have very little to do with the European Central Bank or the balance of trade. Its origins will lie in the way Europe 'gives a place in the sun to Europe's smaller and middle-sized nations', and by implication a diminished place to the post-imperial big cheeses. Such a climate of ordinariness would have a different Europe inherent within it – anti-puissant, Swiss rather than Great, and devoted to cultivation of its own assorted gardens.

In the vistas of Greatness and *rayonnement*, however, this is the sort of change that gets noticed only to be scorned. It is unworthy of *francité* and Britishness alike.

Happily, in *Les infortunes de la République*, Jean-Marie Colombani has simultaneously given both French and European analysis a very different and much more serious spectrum to work with. The subtitle of the present book was inspired by Mr Colombani's reflections on France, from the point of view of a Corsican. What these 'misfortunes of the Republic' depicts is a France not so much alternative to, as evidently parallel with the anachronistic structure and statist attitudes of late 'Britain'. Although Editor of *Le Monde*, France's most important newspaper, Mr Colombani also perceives his adopted country from a deeply felt peripheral angle, and is unsparing of the Republic's insensate centralising conceit and rigidity. The 'Corsican problem' is in truth the problem of France (he states firmly at the beginning of his book) and reflects the central élite's will to maintain at all costs a grandiose early-modern rôle:

> France . . . as the bearer of a grander idea, rather like the United States. It has always conceived its political construction not as a pragmatic means for cohabitation and adaptation to changes, but as a privileged access to universality, a building block of the universal Republic, a wonderful machine for forcing individual wills into legal conformity. We may not be better than anyone else. But our ideals must always be greater than those of our neighbours.

Hence the unshakeable conviction that 'republican France has something to tell the world', preferably (but not indispensably) via a Europe which has been previously galvanised by '*le projet français*'. Deriving from De Gaulle's resurrection of Frenchness in the Fifth Republic, this is a rough equivalent of the Thatcher and Blair 'projects' by which the British have been bewitched and hounded since 1979. It entails the utter necessity of keeping Corsica, Brittany, Alsace and all other possibly restive provinces. 'Losing Corsica would be the beginning of the end', as the neo-Republican Jean-Pierre Chevènement has put it – echoing (to British ears) the diatribes of Tam Dalyell, Peter Hitchens, and so many others.

And indeed, inability to keep *'votre petit Corse'* (as apparently President Mitterrand enjoyed saying) within France's Project might throw doubt on vehicle and destination alike. The majority of individual French men and women might be unconcerned by the 'loss' – just as most English would be about Scottish independence. But this is unimportant. What counts is that less-than-Universal status would then become a definite possibility *for the élites of the Republic*. That would lead to loss of Centre charisma, crippling doubts about Presidential autocracy, mounting 'regional' ambitions, and the disquietude of a country which remains (Republican mythology notwithstanding) the most diverse in Western Europe.[52]

Colombani's recommendation in *Les infortunes* amounts to the frank abandonment of this manic Republicanism. He argues for a retreat from Jacobinism to a flexible 'regionalism', which he associates with Tocqueville and the traditions of the pre-1792 Gironde. The reforms in Corsica – analogous to UK Devolution – led to the 'Matignon process', a supposed development of stable, shared responsibilities between Paris and the island. It is striking how the same language is employed under both states. In the UK too, all official apologies for setting up sub-state authority have insisted

---

52 French demographer and social analyst Emmanuel Todd has underlined this point in a number of recent works, most strongly in *La diversité du monde: famille et modernité* (1999). The devout centralism of Parisian authority is like a permanent spell meant to keep such diversity in its place – its non-political place. Primitive magic is thus common to both these early-modern states, although 'unwritten' in one and spelt out in elaborate constitutional forms by the other.

upon 'process' as the appropriate, open-minded description of their activities. The implication seems to be a central power permanently and benevolently open to reasonable readjustments and concessions – provided it controls the definition of 'reason'. Endlessly extolled 'Process' is an excellent thing, in fact, provided it never arrives anywhere.

Mr Colombani does not argue for Corsican independence, but his conclusion is none the less revealingly more radical than that of most Westminster pundits. A Sixth Republic is required, he asserts, within which a self-governing Corsica could become a model, rather than a harbinger of loss and decline. In other words, vital changes are needed at the centre, not on the periphery alone. *Les infortunes* pleads for a different, more plural France renouncing its unitarist pretences and central conceits. France as just another European country, in fact – or more accurately an *assemblage* or constellation of 'countries', rather than the navel of modernity itself. [53]

But his book also conveys vividly the difficulty of advancing such a view in France. There is a powerful bloc of reactionaries utterly devoted to the maintenance of Republican élitism – not just their own jobs, but what those positions mean (or are supposed to mean): the true national interest. However contrasting their recipes may be, Left and Right do tend to remain united on the matter of *grandeur*. Giving up on that inherited 'certain idea of France' would mean subordination and the same kind of

---

53 Essentially the same point has now been expressed in a formal movement for a Sixth Republic. 'C6R', a movement analogous to Britain's Charter 88, appealed for a range of reforms in the run-up to the forthcoming elections in France. Their Open Letter foresees 'a crisis of trust so severe that our fellow citizens have committed themselves to a provocative voting strike, of which democracy is the first victim'. An end to dual mandates, a call for open government, proportional representation in local elections – the similarities are striking. So is the rhetorical conclusion: 'Our Republic, long presented as a model, has become the subject of international ridicule, riddled as it is with corruption, reform breakdowns and loss of authority . . .' (website: www.c6r-fr.org).

defeat as dropping the metaphorical 'Great' out of 'Britain'. The same spec-
tre of prostration is then unleashed: the ascendancy of Germany, or of
America, or of an unrestrained and faceless capitalism ready to fall upon
a divided or 'regionalised' Europe.

In short, the misfortunes of Jacques Chirac's Republic are not after all
so profoundly different from those of Tony Blair's Kingdom across the
Channel. There are common European themes here, which merit far more
attention than those which have recently surfaced in recent and largely
hypocritical debates about the Euro-currency. Chancellor Brown's 'Five
Conditions' for UK participation have been intended (successfully) as a
deliberate distraction from the political problems of European Union.
The distraction was necessary because no 'British' end-phase state can
possibly consider a democratic Union in which the smaller states prevail,
indifferent (or even hostile) to world-power pretensions and Leadership.

In 2004 there will be a European Union conference which, following upon
the Nice Treaty, cannot avoid the question of a European constitution. How
on earth can the Pariah of 2001 insert itself into a debate of that sort?
Devolution has made some difference: Scotland, Wales and the Northern
Ireland of the Peace Process could (for instance) easily insert themselves into
the new Colloquium of the Regions. But what about England, neither political nation nor plausible 'region', yet also devoid of internal regions? How can
a customary constitution be formally integrated into a new (and presumably
extremely 'written', and argued out) framework for European identity?

In his great historical account of European formation, *The European
Rescue of the Nation-state*, Alan Milward argued that the first 'European
Community' was by no means a straightforward attempt to transcend
and leave behind 'the nation-state' of the 1950s. It was intended above all to
restore national statehood in Western Europe after the unique defeats and
humiliations which most of them had suffered between 1939 and 1945.
However, restoration was now a common task, more easily achieved by

closer collaboration and acceptance of a common secular religion: 'Europe'. Jean Monnet and the other 'European Saints' formulated and preached this faith, adding primarily economic arguments to a powerful popular reaction against the inter-war nationalism and protectionism perceived as responsible for the disaster.

The restoration was successful, and the saintly vision was that revived states would be habituated to common action, legislation and markets. A momentum would be set up from which some form of common or joint statehood would emerge. This was all under what Perry Anderson later called 'the sign of the interim' – a developing, sometimes contradictory process which unforeseeable events would also help to advance (or possibly arrest). But the principal difficulty of the interim was the huge disparities among the polities that it sought to bridge. In time, these came to include one of the victors of 1945, the United Kingdom, and the restored empire of Republican France. Had European Union been attempted solely by the defeated and the occupied, or by the smaller countries like Belgium, Luxembourg, Portugal, Denmark and Ireland, then its chances of confederation would have been much stronger.

Political unity might have advanced more rapidly, for reasons obvious in the smaller states. They identified their national identities with the grander project, perceiving it as increment rather than challenge or sacrifice. They could go on 'being themselves' *and* become more influential simultaneously. The greater space of Europe represented opportunity and adventure, comparable to that of America or Australia, rather than retrenchment and resignation. They did not have to stay 'great': union or federation represented a future possibility of greatness, not the preservation of past epics and mythical centrality.

When British rulers face the dire prospect of falling into ordinariness, they seem to be imagining a cul-de-sac: sheer loss, near-extinction, never 'counting' for anything again. If they abandon their coinage, their inherited identity will somehow evaporate with it. Being 'like everyone else' is felt as next to extinction – conquest by roundabout, non-military means. Like Russia, Serbia and France, Great Britain can never be 'small' in this ideological sense. Europe is thus interpreted primarily as an invitation to insignificance, the final sacrifice of exceptionality. Small, naturally insignificant peoples may have different views; but for a multinational, naturally out-reaching people genetically endowed with *rayonnement,* all cession of Sovereignty is a sort of death.

The renewal of this style of nationalism was what the June 2001 election was about, both for government and opposition. New Labour and Conservatism have become bands of Greatness-delinquents, down-at-heel ex-supremos in whom their followers have really lost faith. Yet no other option is made available by a cramped system of power; one can only continue supporting 'them' by routine and indurate custom. Their demeaning persistence prevents alternatives from arising (and is of course intended to do so). The future of the archipelago lies in the direction sketched out by Norman Davies: a collection of (relatively) small independent or near-independent states, eight or nine in number, with a collective mutual interest in good relations, and a variety of common links to the European Union – above all on the level of law, common rights and juridical practice.

In fact the British–Irish 'ethnos' (in the Ancient Greek sense) could find a new role as a test-bed of novel relationships within European Union.[54]

---

54 Among the city-state Greeks an 'ethnos' was the approximately common customs, discourse and observances of a group or 'family' of independent states – not the indwelling *Geist* of differentiation fantasized by nineteenth- and twentieth- century nationalists. Political independence was perfectly compatible with valuing and sharing cultural and other attributes on a wider scene – elements of 'civil society', as many would say today. See M.I. Finley's essay 'The Ancient Greeks and Their Nation', in *The Use and Abuse of History* (Viking Press 1975).

This is exactly what (although partly in spite of itself) the United Kingdom and Ireland already began to attempt in 1997–98, with the Belfast Agreement. If that initiative fails it will be the fault of 'Britain', not of mob violence and narrow nationalism (as will undoubtedly be claimed). Britishness on the streets in Orange shape, plus Britishness at large, in the shape of the Kingdom's final inability to settle accounts with those who cling to it. De Gaulle did this with the Algerian *pied-noirs*, by founding a new Republic. But Westminster under Blair seems to have less and less intention of founding a new constitutional Kingdom.

The former would-be great states, Germany and Italy, were forced after defeat and occupation to discover an analogous road to recovery, via federal and regional government inside the Treaty of Rome. 'Restoration' for them (as for Spain after Franco's death) was no return to quasi-imperial centrality and refurbished grandeur. But for the French and British states, this is exactly what remains at stake. Their ruling strata have always wanted to use Europe, not to join it: the French by political captaincy of the emerging Community, the British by keeping it at arm's length in order to guarantee their outreach capitalism and *le grand large.* Their presence in the Union has made sure that (in Larry Siedentop's influential recent account) 'there is no viable model' of European polity corresponding to the economy of a Central Bank and the common currency.[55]

Naturally, history does not turn back at the behest of anachronisms like the Fifth Republic and Britain's Reliquary-Kingdom. The post-Cold War reformation of European societies into a smaller, more diverse pattern is proceeding in any case. In this perspective, the UK election of June 2001 was only a minor if dismal setback. It did some damage, and probably set the stage for a good deal more over the coming decade. But this is also

---

55 Larry Siedentop, *Democracy in Europe* (new edition, Penguin 2001).

likely to be redressed by Scottish independence, by more authentic autonomy in Wales, and a more consequent (and more constitutional)
awakening of English identity. However difficult the political problems
these changes pose for Europe, none of the successor entities is likely to
suffer from 'Europhobia', the festering curse of Ukania *in extremis*. They
are more likely to seek positive support from Europe, along the general
lines suggested by Göran Therborn in his 'Europe in the Twenty-first
Century'.[56]

The scenarios he imagines there are 'A Second West Germany, or
Scandinavia Enlarged?' His underlying point is that *both* these paths mean
that 'Europe is unlikely to become a normative power, telling other parts of
the world what political, economic and social institutions they should
have'. What he means is that there is (mercifully) no chance whatever of
Europe becoming a larger France or Great Britain. As Germany writ large,
Europe would become a major economic force in the neo-liberal world,
requiring 'the constant sharpening of a competitive edge on a long economic blade'. It must be doubtful if this will be sustainable without a
parallel political edge (which Germany shows no signs of evolving). By
contrast 'the Scandinavian model needs only the capacity for competitive
sharpness in certain niche fields, and the maintenance of a certain amount
of relative prosperity'. Therborn favours this second, more modest vision,
as (it will be plain by now) does the author of this book. 'I would hazard',
he concludes, 'that, at least by the second half of the twenty-first century,
the best Europeans can hope for is to constitute a nice, decent periphery of
the world, with little power but some good ideas.'

---

56 *The Question of Europe*, edited by Peter Gowan and Perry Anderson (Verso 1997)
Chapter 22, pp. 357–84.

12 DR BRITAIN AND MR ENGLAND, OR: MORE DIRTY POOL?

From my window I see the guttering
of an antiquated house of crumbling wood,
weighed down by layers of tiles.
Sometimes swallows land there,
on its roof covered with miserable repairs,
patches of tar and cement over apex and joints,
the leading worn away by rain and snow.
Yet the rotting roof-tree still holds up.

And not without joy I think that,
One day soon – no matter
I'm not there to see it – one single bird will land,
in a second of time, and
the whole lot will fall into the void, irreparably;
while the bird flies free.

Franco Fortini, 'The Eaves' in *Una volta*
per sempre [Once and for All] (1978)

During the 2001 electoral campaign (as for years before) political journalists puzzled over the personality of Tony Blair. As we have seen, few looking from outside doubted that something ominous was under way. But what was its connection with the tensely smiling personality of New Labour's Leader? One of the most suspicious, and tenacious, of such observers was the *New Yorker*'s Joe Klein, for example (already cited earlier). He commented after a day on the campaign trail:

> Blair does have a rather synthetic quality, 'A man without a hinterland'
> Roderick Nye, the policy director for the Tories, says. And there is an
> indescribable something missing from his public persona . . . He
> recently acknowledged enjoying 'The Simpsons'. But he always leaves
> one wondering if moments like the 'Simpsons' revelation are, somehow,
> tactical – the latest planned attempt at humanization. (*New Yorker*,
> 4 June 2001)

He compares Blair to President Clinton in this respect. However comparable in policy terms, he says, the two remain oceans apart as public
personae. On election day itself the *Guardian* published another attempt by
Klein at reading the oracle:

> Even now, as he approaches a likely second landslide, no one seems to
> know how Tony Blair feels as a person or, more to the point, who he is.
> This is both extraordinary and mystifying. He is about as familiar as a
> public figure can be. We know that he is religious . . . But there remains
> an ineffable something missing. There is an antiseptic, impenetrable,
> stainless-steel brightness to Blair. There are no rough edges, few edges of
> any sort . . . (*Guardian*, 7 June 2001, *G2* section)

These are very perceptive comments, but they may also be out of focus.
The absence of a readable 'hinterland' and of 'rough edges', spontaneity
somehow rendered contrived or deliberate, a somewhat super-human
demeanour salted by affectations of impulse or immediacy: these are
indeed enigmatic as individual traits. However, they are also perfect
descriptions of *Britishness*. They seem to delineate a social, collective ethos
rather than personal idiosyncracies.

The identity they replicate is also rather outdated: this is a 'Britishness'
that used to be, rather than the confusion of the present. But there may be
good reasons for that. Like Blair's increasingly prominent religiosity, it

may still be felt as a necessary condition of acceptability. After all, we know political parties are among the most conservative of social bodies, and in this case they inhabit the most long-lived and conservative of states. The latter's multi-layered narratives compel the present to embody the past – however much 'radicalism' is spouted at the same time. Personal rigidity is one possible form of such embodiment.

Imperturbability in command was a celebrated trait of the former ruling class. It was strongly linked to the secondary significance of Britain's 'hinterland'. Ruling cadres of course came from somewhere – their own patch of turf, one or other 'British' country – but command-structure homogeneity was for centuries far more important. There was a *political* sense in which Ellis Wasson's 'two thousand five hundred' of the UK *ancien régime* came from nowhere – or were located in the same 'British' dimension (*Born to Rule*: see earlier note). This was one of the secrets of overseas extension, including 'indirect rule', and (before that) of the post-1688 archipelago. Tony Blair incarnates a lot of that world-view, but of course does so also in the manner of the present: personally, with a measure of off-handedness which always risks appearing con-trived or 'trendy'. Yet that too is inevitable: it rings false, yet without it he would simply sound outdated – straight out of the pre-Thatcher world, as it were.

The effect is indeed that of a magician who has made a compact with a ghost – the haunting presence of a spirit, 'elusive' mainly in the sense of significantly detached from interlocutors and the contemporary public. Yet that detachment also supplies a certain leverage over his audience. What the mixture of phlegm and steeliness does is to create a space of surmise. Beholders are usually tempted to think that if they behave correctly, then he might still produce what they want out of the enigmatic hat. Blair never quite escapes the suspicion of not quite being himself – as distinct from *pretending* to be his own self. But this edgelessness can also be interpreted as a constantly moving promise. Those Liberal commentators who on the 6th and 7th of June ended up by urging readers to vote New Labour (in spite of everything, gritting their teeth, etc.) did so entirely in those terms: '*He may yet still . . .*' (and so forth).

'Identity' in this sense is a fusion of the personal and the social, which also means 'national'. Nobody ever doubted for a second that Mrs Thatcher or John Major were *English*, however loudly they orated in the name of Britain. No one would see Gordon Brown as other than Scottish, however hard he may yet fight for the Union. The Welshness of former party Leader Neil Kinnock was legendary, even though he opposed Welsh Devolution as expensive parochialism. But Tony Blair? The absent or fog-shrouded hinterland means that he is somehow just 'British', or possibly English-British – enough of the former to reassure, but with the emphasis strongly on the latter. This is surely the source of that 'synthetic' dimension Klein identifies.

'Britain' is of course by definition a nationless identity. Different components of it tend to project on to it what they wish or need to see. Immigrants hope 'nationless' means (or can be made to mean) 'multi-national', or 'multi-cultural'. Fascists hope it means 'racial', a connection to the figurative common blood of Aryanism. Middle-Englanders trust that it will go on just meaning what it used to mean, 'for all practical purposes'. The Scottish, Welsh and Ulster-Unionist servants of synthetic statehood want it above all to go on including *them* – which it can still do, they feel, though only if everybody is kept in line and given injections of British backbone.

No doubt much in Blair's personal story contributed to today's persona. John Rentoul's biography gives a good account of the family background: the adopted identity on his father Leo's side, and the Irish, Scottish and North-Eastern strains in his childhood formation. He was sent to Fettes Public School in Edinburgh – 'essentially an English private school in Scotland', as Rentoul puts it, 'where as many boys were Anglicans as Church of Scotland'.[57] Ideology was prominent in the family: Ultra-Protestantism (on his mother's side), Communist Party Marxism (the father's foster-parents), and the strident Conservatism to which his father eventually moved. The Fettes ordeal was 'finished' in Oxford, where with a rock band he underwent a famous *Zeitgeist* moment of adaptation, before a legal degree and training with 'Derry Irvine' (Lord Irvine of Lairg). In an early profile of Blair in *Atlantic Monthly* (1996) Geoffrey Wheatcroft speculated that his Donegal-Protestant origins might still retain some influence, in the sense that 'the cause of Irish nationalism would get no more of a hearing from a Blair government than from John Major's' (but it should be recalled this was two years before the Belfast Agreement).

However Blair's background should now be deciphered, it is clearly very 'British' in a cross-national sense. No one is likely either to dispute this or to criticise it in itself. From the cross-hatching of such varied inputs, depths may emerge, as well as shallow mix-ups or uncertainties. But in Blair's case the depths remain speculative; what Joe Klein and everyone else can sense is a kind of muscular shallowness. A leadership *persona* is formed by the synthesis of such factors with institutional constraints – in this case, the ultra-Great-Brit Labour Party, which just as Blair joined up was discovering that it could lose its Socialism a lot easier than its Britishness. Wheatcroft thought in 1996 that Blair was driven mainly by hatred of the Old Labour Party, as typified by Tony Benn and Dennis Skinner. Whether or not that is correct, Labour certainly soon needed a figurehead shaped

---

57 John Rentoul, *Tony Blair, Prime Minister* (Little, Brown 2001). The author adds: 'Blair regards himself as English, although when he described himself thus in the Commons he corrected himself, first to say "Well, born in Scotland but brought up in England", then to declare, "I'm British and proud to be British"' (p. 14).

strongly for Britain, and relatively uncontaminated by 'old-fashioned' Socialist piety. And in Tony Blair, it did find (so to speak) Dr Jekyll without Mr Hyde: a rare chameleon capable of 'fronting' the Movement's transformation into the neo-liberal world bequeathed by Mrs Thatcher, and of rebuilding its national role there. More precisely, of rebuilding as much as possible of the *traditional* national role: 'standing up for Britain' (etc.).

The factors which made Blair ideal for New Labour should also help to dispel worry about what he may turn into. After the election, for example, we find one of Scotland's finest political analysts still perplexed by the problem. 'Will the Real Tony Blair Stand Up?' Iain Macwhirter asked in the *Sunday Herald* (10 June). 'It is strange and a little scary,' he comments, 'that we know so little about the Prime Minister even after electing him with two landslides'. He continues:

> In the past, Tony Blair perhaps felt that he had to be all things to all men – and women. That to make Labour electable it had to win *Sun* readers as well as the *Guardian*'s. But after Landslide 2 he has no longer any excuse for ideological evasion . . . [and] . . . can no longer allow his party and personality to look as if they are a media creation. He now has to walk the walk. And this he intends to do.

Labour is going to get much tougher, he concludes. I'm sure this is right. But I doubt if it will be because the 'real' Blair finally emerges. What we have seen so far is what we are likely to go on getting. It is unlikely that some alter ego is waiting to pounce. But what *has* emerged, in intensified and more threatening form since the election, is a seriously threatened Britishness. The Leader of New Labour is bound to take that 'personally'. Quite apart from the vexing dilemma of the Euro-currency referendum (which will really have to be won *in all four countries* of the UK), there is the question of the Barnett Formula for financial carve-ups, and that of how to win the next elections in Scotland and Wales, while keeping the Northern Ireland Agreement alive. All these will require a sustained barrage of no-nonsense and no-surrender Unionism from the Prime Minister and his watchdogs – and notably from his Scottish contingent.

Both politically and personally, therefore, Tony Blair is essentially a vehicle of 'transformism': the same *trasformismo* as Stuart Hall originally identified in the analysis quoted earlier. That is, the mechanism of theft and adaptation by which Left becomes Right, or vice versa, always in the name of the State and of an abstractly idealised 'community' made to stand in for the nation. No longer possible without Devolution, this New Labour retread has demanded in compensation an ultra-British accentuation of the dominant climate, and a corresponding change in popular attitudes – precisely what the aggravated, even hysterical, populism of the first New Labour government has been seeking to achieve.

The Greenwich Dome was intended to be a mighty landmark for that direction in affairs – the enduring symbol of a United Kingdom reborn and ready for another century. As the whole world knows, it was a farce. There was nothing – or nothing suitable – to fill it with. Like 'Britain', its historic contents and purpose had been lost, and no amount of money and cultural striving could put them back again. So it turned almost at once into a poison sac, an abscess of miserable disputes and corrupt handouts which was miraculously kept more or less out of view during the recent electoral campaign. 'Dr Britain' was then triumphantly reinstalled on a quarter of the votes. So the poison will have at least four more years, and quite possibly nine or ten, to slowly fill the whole bloodstream of the British state-nation.

In retrospect one may also see the sense of the Blair–Brown conundrum more clearly. Whether or not they arrived at some kind of compact about leadership after John Smith's death, the choice was never between England

and Scotland. For that to happen, English identity would have had to be far more politically formulated. It is now somewhat more discernible, but in the mid-1990s remained below the horizon for practical fellows like these. After John Smith, Labour may indeed have been chary about another Scottish leader; but the quandary was conveniently resolved by Blair's ostentatious Britishness. It is doubtful if many wanted an English captain in any emphatic or ethnic sense. Absence of 'hinterland' and cloudy religiosity were much safer, and made up for suspicions of shallowness or brashness.

What was safer then is probably even more necessary now. 'England' has become more politically salient, and the Scottish Parliament is likely to challenge the economic basis of the 1998 Scotland Act – the fiscal dependency of the block grant. But in the foreseeable future, these and other problems seem likely to underwrite Tony Blair's leadership rather than demolish it. Who else in the ranks of New Labour can 'speak for Britain' in just his easy fashion? None of the Westminster Scots, for sure. Soon, they will all be preoccupied with 'saving the Union', a project even more hopeless than the Millennium Dome. But this does not mean that Blairism will not invest heavily in it during its second term of office.

How likely this is can be seen from the much-publicised 'Touchstone Issues' memorandum leaked to the *Times* in July 2000. The Downing Street document sought to identify 'strategic' themes capable of linking together disparate government policies and ideas. It was looking forward to the next election, and to the years which might follow. These themes should 'combine "on your side" issues with toughness and *standing up for Britain*', it argued. 'The family' and being harder on asylum-seeking immigrants figure prominently in a formula meant to put right any 'sense that the government – and this even applies to me – are somehow *out of touch with gut British instincts*'. In his survey of recent constitutional thinking, John Morrison comments that: 'The "touchstone issues" memo is a spine-chilling insight into Blair's mind. The level of defence spending is to be determined not by any objective need but by the Prime Minister's desire to be seen to be standing up for Britain'.[58]

In a sombre prospect written just as the election campaign got under way, George Walden saw that 'the election will be an insult to any self-respecting voter – man-made imbecility against a background of natural disaster'. The countryside plague would eventually come to an end, but what he called *cultural* foot-and-mouth will be less easily eradicated. It seems to be rooted in the state itself, and has now acquired a sense of fatal inevitability. Britain is now coming to *mean* 'a combination of priggery and demagoguery, of High Church and low methods . . . insupportable, but it seems we are going to have to put up with it.'[59]

---

58 The Memorandum is reproduced in the last chapter of Morrison's book *Reforming Britain*, 'The D-Word', pp. 495–537 (italicisation added). Morrison concludes that Blair's 'Holy Grail' is a style of cross-class and pragmatic politics rooted in moral and religious factors rather than political or constitutional ones. This leads to a fixation on *community* which in practice can only be manifested in homogeneously 'British' terms. Hence all assaults on British communitarianism must be sternly repelled. They are in effect assaults on people like Tony Blair. As former Liberal-Democrat leader Paddy Ashdown puts it: 'The real thing he believes in is that Britain will be okay if it is governed by decent people. By which he means "people like me". He admires people who do tough things to bring their countries up to date, without necessarily assessing whether the "up to date" means more democratic or not . . .' (*Reforming Britain*, pp. 536–7). In 1997 this meant a perfectly visible identification with some aspects of Mrs Thatcher's régime. In 2002 it has come to imply an equivalent sympathy with Silvio Berlusconi and President George W. Bush.

59 George Walden, 'Along the Right Lines', *Times Literary Supplement*, 'Commentary', 11 May 2001.

EPILOGUE 2002

'Globalisation' is now taken to be the motive force of historical destiny . . . One is struck by the feeling of powerlessness which typifies this period, finding expression in a hundred variants of one single ideology, the supposed inevitability of economic processes. The powerlessness of states, of nations and of ruling classes has produced a spiritual abasement in paradoxical contrast to the same period's Promethean technological advances . . .

Emmanuel Todd, *L'illusion économique: essai sur la stagnation des sociétés dévelopées* (Gallimard, 1997), p. 14

Globalisation involves a lot more than *One Market Under God* (to quote the title of Thomas Frank's recent and delightful polemic, 2001). As Emmanuel Todd has shown in his *L'illusion économique*, it has depended so far upon the dissemination of a secular faith, the new monotheism of cure-all Free Trade, or marketolatry. During the 1980s and 1990s, political economy in the older, classical sense was deserted for this skeletal and philistine parody. A supposed dissolution of the 'nation-state' left economic forces as the sole agency of development and advance. Abandonment of political will-power compelled a displacement into an improbable alternative: the 'realism' of management boards, growth (or decline) tables, and share or property ownership. Propagated unceasingly by a zealotic and worldwide clerisy of economists, journalists, think-tanks and politicians, this faith then became almost the 'common sense' of the initial phase of globalisation that followed the collapse of Communism in the 1980s.

Thus economism replaced economics. The dismal science gave way to a dismally englobing *Weltanschauung*, in which 'economic man' was elevated from useful fellow to despicable tyrant, and most governments found themselves driven towards becoming his lickspittle accomplices. Competition in a free, global market was made the unique yardstick of accomplishment and status, and the unbending disciplinarian of antediluvian nonsense like community, happiness, equality and culture. The new common sense perceived free enterprise not merely as one necessary condition of progress, but as the practically sufficient condition of everything else. The notorious complexity of societal cause-and-effect was narrowed down by this superstition into a single conduit. As the surviving signpost to both individual and social salvation, global economism has taken over from, and transcended in absurdity, all humankind's antecedent fixations: Jesus Christ, the Word of Allah, Buddha, Karl Marx.

British New Labour is but a minor actor in this broader tragi-comedy. The reaffirmation of Blair's Third Way in June 2001 was only one parochial episode, an example among hundreds of how post-Cold War neo-liberalism continues, and of the disaffection and malaise now generated by its spread. Most of the foregoing has been concerned with the specific machinery of that episode – that is, with the prolonged hangover of Britishness, the folklore of its afterlife, and the pathology of its fake modernisation. I hope that such detail has not distracted attention too much from the grander issue at stake here, the question of Emmanuel Todd's 'powerlessness'. It certainly ought not to. For alas, the political backwardness of UK constitutionalism is typical, as well as being highly peculiar.

Blair's re-coronation in June 2001 was of course massively rooted in the UK's nineteenth-century national identity. But it also relied upon the still unfolding, if now stumbling, *Zeitgeist* of marketolatry and 'deregulation'. The weight of the British dead generations has been consistently amplified by certain general and unrelenting conditions of the present. Indeed Her

Majesty's Unwritten Constitution is in part preserved by these general circumstances of political debility and democratic deficit. In the same essay, Todd tellingly contrasts the climate of today with that attending past scientific and economic breakthroughs. In their time, simpler devices like the book, the steam-engine, internal combustion and electric power brought in their wake vaulting ambitions, imperial dreams and a sense of Utopia. How on earth can it be that the information revolution, bio-science, nano-technology and space-exploration now induce mass stupefaction, the belittlement of politics and a mounting conviction that 'there is no such thing as "society"'? The scale of real change and possibility calls for Prometheus; instead of which, the globe is suffering Blair, Bush, *Big Brother*, Berlusconi and Australia's John Howard.

The UK's absurd microcosm rests upon the persistence of an *ancien régime*. But then, *so does the whole macrocosm of neo-liberalism*. People have generally (and thankfully) forgotten the Armaggedon whose menace petrified the world from the 1950s to the end of the 1980s. But that past has not forgotten them. Though small by holocaust standards, the terrorist attacks of 11 September 2001 were enough to reanimate its shade, and many of its attitudes.

For most of the past century, it was assumed that the single fate in store for mankind would be the consequence of such an apocalyptic struggle, almost certainly meaning vast and indiscriminate destruction. One imperium or another would win out militarily, possibly even at the risk of species-extinction or at least its modification through 'nuclear winter'. Then the victors would impose their global political formula. Since the 1980s that expectation has of course evaporated. People have all too readily forgotten how pervasive and crushing it was, and today's students find it hard to imagine what such a clammy, unrelenting grip was like. They have inherited its devastating cramp, with little understanding of what first froze the sinews.

Yet astoundingly little sense of liberation accompanied this dark angel's fall, in 1988 and 1989. 'Globalisation' in the current sense derived mainly, I would argue almost entirely, from that moment: that is, from the profound sense of a single fate, no longer challengeable by any real alternative. One may naturally trace and identify all sorts of precursors, in earlier patterns of commerce, conquest and development. However, these proceeded across a globe either partly unknown, or deeply divided. None had anything approaching the finality of the 'Second World's' fall.

Yet no jubilee marked this colossal shift – the signal of our species' final command of its world, comparable to the invention of agriculture, or of the written word. Was not the drear mediocrity and privatisation-mania of the present day presaged by that earlier absence of celebration? In retrospect, it is as if the world lapsed glumly into neo-liberalism, rather than bursting heroically forth to claim it. Even at that time – under Yeltsin, Thatcher, Mitterrand and the earlier George Bush – free-trade mania somehow triumphed by default. It was just there, already ineluctable, rather than being the fruit of cultural battles, or of a virtuous political revolution. Why was this?

While nobody doubts that being worked over by 'market forces' was better than being blown up or irradiated, it remained disconcertingly like a change in the weather rather than a new age. The ideological reign of *homo economicus* crept in the world's back door, and made itself at home *sans cérémonie*. He placed quietly on the table his order for the days to come: Freedom is essentially free enterprise, economics alone is real, and all else is appearance, shadow or consequence. At its worst (most of the time) it amounted to claiming that capitalism's 'economic man' was simply natural. With the Fall of Communism, Nature had come in to her own. Nobody expected her Messiah to be Milton Friedman; but there he was.

The clammy triumph of this 'Nature' was in truth only the glacial deposit of the generation before: the slowest-thawing part of the terrorised immobilism that held sway between the 1950s and the later 1980s. In 1945, the victorious powers had claimed the collective mantle of 'democracy'. Even then, it might have been more accurate to say that Great-Russian and Atlantic-seaboard nationalisms had combined to smash Fascism. However, to the victors went the ideological spoils as well. In 1939–40 even the old British and French Empires, even Stalin's cruel parody of Socialism, had been preferable to Aryan conquest – and after 1945, what they said went.

> The individuals composing the ruling class possess among other things consciousness, and therefore think. Insofar, therefore, as they rule as a class and determine the extent and compass of an epoch, it is self-evident that they do this in its whole range, hence among other things rule also as thinkers, as producers of ideas, and regulate the production and distribution of the ideas of their age; thus their ideas are the ruling ideas of the epoch.[60]

What held for Marx's 'German ideology' in 1846 is true of globalisation's formative epoch. And the 'eternal law' of the latter has been overwhelmingly, one-sidedly economic. The combination of political conservatism and the Cold War formed this irresistible mould.

Triumphant powers experience no need for constitutional change or political reform, they can't help perceiving themselves as all-round successes, vindicated by history. However, what actually triumphed in 1945 was a bewildering set of Atlantic seaboard political antiques. The bright new, post-fascist world may have been deserving of equally new democracies. What it got was the half-restored old furniture of the eighteenth century. Winston Churchill's British state dated from the 1640–88 era, and

---

60 Karl Marx and Friedrich Engels, *The German Ideology* (1846), Electric Book Company CD edition, 1997.

Roosevelt's American Constitution from the 1790s. The France restored by De Gaulle's wartime leadership was the resurrection of a centralised polity whose structure went back to long before the Third (then the Fourth) Republic. It derived from 1790s Jacobinism, which itself partly replicated centuries of Absolute Monarchy. Everyone knows the jokes about democracy being the least bad form of state; but a sour codicil can also be considered: it may be just a little more less-bad if not *also* centuries behind the times.

And yet, these antiques were to endure into the following century. The victorious crocks of the Atlantic seaboard remain with us in 2002, still trumpeting their alibis of life everlasting (with or without God – and still on the whole more with than without). They continue to 'lead the West', and hence the world. In the millenial year of 2000 the United States constitution failed to elect George W. Bush as President; as a result of which not only did Bush become President, he now leads the Free World in a Crusade against Terrorism. Still pining for President Reagan's Evil Empire, he has forged a clumsy substitute, an 'Axis of Evil' justifying both rearmament and Godly values. In 2001 – as we have seen – the Westminster Constitution secured the overwhelming return of Tony Blair on significantly less than one quarter of the registered vote, with 40 per cent of abstentions. Yet this has been enough to turn the man into more than just another British Premier. It has allowed him to set up as the very pivot and schoolmaster of Global Democracy, an ever-travelling salesman of Third Way mysticism.

Such longevity is in part accounted for by the way that one redemption followed upon another. 1945 was soon followed by 1948, and the descent of the Iron Curtain. The dominant Western states were immediately and unanswerably politically superior to the totalitarian dictatorships across the divide. Already *de trop*, political revolution became less and less thinkable. Just as even the British and French Empires had been preferable to

Nazism, so their archaic successors remained incomparably preferable to Stalinist, and then to Maoist, tyranny. Even in the most tolerable zones of Communism, like Yugoslavia, democracy remained a farce.

Where radical politics was disallowed in this way, and even reform became highly suspect, economics naturally took over. Third World and anti-colonial revolts were unstoppable after 1945; however, they remained regimentable. The effective choice was between Socialist and capitalist economic systems – both vulgarised and packaged to suit. Politics came with the Accessories kit, like an early graphic interface. The political economy of Adam Smith and J.M. Keynes gave way to the economistic politics of the last third of the twentieth century. Freedom – the victorious banner of 1945 – shrivelled into free enterprise. A liberal society became identified with free-range capitalism, deregulation and return towards a minimalist or 'night-watchman' state. Thus the globe ended up in double-locked conservative arthritis. Stalinism and neo-liberalism together drained innovatory politics out of both sides in the Cold War. While the East foundered in Talmudic misreadings of historical materialism, the West reverted to *laisser-faire* reborn, and the fatalism of the bottom line. Todd's 'economic illusion' was common to both sides. And short of war, this contest of crazed economisms was capable only of an economic dénouement – the sordid, half-hearted triumph of one version or the other of *homo economicus*.

In UK terms, the resultant fusion of political archaism with capitalist prosperity was represented by Margaret Thatcher. In America, it was exemplified by Nixon and Reagan, but above all by the monstrous figure of Henry Kissinger: the true man of the age, a resurgent *Geist* of transplanted traditionalism, conserved and bloated into devious and ruthless control of the new – Marx's 'sorcerer' of bourgeois modernity in the flesh, harnessing the unchained forces of production to the service of immovable élites, militarism and decrepit forms of the state. On both sides of the Atlantic, the Left collapsed under his new 'eternal law', gargling the bitter snake-oil of political impotence and collective incompetence.

There was an effective moratorium on *political* development by both parties to the Great Contest. Among Free-Worlders, the tried-and-tested bathchairs of Old Glory, Westminsterism and *La République Une et Indivisible* remained unchallengeable, except by cranks and 'subversives'. The latter did attempt revolt in 1968, the single interlude of sanity in this whole epoch. Youngsters and dissidents refused to credit that social and cultural emancipation could really go on cohabiting with De Gaulle, Nixon and Harold Wilson. They were quickly disabused, where necessary by force. There was no special logic to the association of capitalism and die-hard conservatism; but no fatal contradiction between them either.

It was a terrified world that had caused retrograde states and paleo-economics to bond, but the joint was quite strong enough to resist tentative, romantic and sectarian assaults – awakenings to politics, rather than matured democracy. A more molecular and longer-prepared alternative was (and still is) needed to recreate the popular sense of agency and possibility. Meanwhile – 'people despise politicians', and for good reasons have come to identify political agency as such with sleaze-economics, furtive despoliation and John K. Galbraith's 'public squalor'.

Globalisation may one day help to liberate societies from this heritage. Unfortunately, the species has been compelled to start globalised life as an extension of it. The recession of the 1970s became still another redemption of capitalist realism, brushing aside the utopian impulses of the previous decade. By the time the failure of Communist development was plain, the ascendancy of capitalism's dismal science had lasted for a generation and a half – quite long enough to seem inevitable, and to build up a vast apparatus of political and media support. This was surely why, when the Eastern systems folded up so rapidly in 1988 and 1989, the Western counterpart filled the vacuum so automatically.

With a kind of leaden inevitability, one variety of economics-worship gave way to the other. Apparatchiks became entrepreneurs overnight, often embracing the credo of Friedrich Von Hayek with the zealous rigidity and passion they had once reserved for that of Lenin. The cure for the ex-Communist East was the installation of capitalist 'civil society' (this is when the term was rediscovered by academics and journalists) with political democracy as its secondary accompaniment, or possibly its long-term effect.

Naturally, the hegemony of economism throughout the West emerged still stronger from this transition. Reaganomics and Thatcherism had seemed excessive to begin with, in the 1970s. Now they appeared so natural that oppositionists settled in the now familiar hypnotised fashion for their own versions of marketolatry and free-trade universalism, using alibis like the Third Way. Blair's New Labour has been a signal example – the triumphant upholding of national exceptionalism by all the routine formulae of globalising astrology and market rhetoric.

Yet by the time New Labour gained office, in the curious, drugged style described earlier, it was plain that this long-term ascendancy of economics was faltering. By the end of 2001 it was visibly falling apart day by day. The timing of the September 2001 outrages was accidental; but they could not help impacting upon a system in disarray, where anti-globalisation had already begun to gather strength and conviction, for reasons owing extremely little to Wahabite Islamicism. In retrospect, it is important to acknowledge how inevitable the hegemony of economism was. But this very inevitability also indicates its boundedness, and its rapidly approaching end. The great sorcerer of modernity is treacherously two-faced, as Marx wrote a century and a half ago: what he inflicts on one generation he may whisk away from the next.

The time of which reactionary economism was the *Geist* launched post-1989 globalisation, and bestowed its initial imprint on the process.

That projection was of a hypostatised entity, a world-market '-ism' possessing independent force and acting almost from without.[61] However, no sooner was this econo-God conjured up than his miserable clay feet were in evidence. The most important of these is the nation. The metaphysics of globalisation, as distinct from the actual extension of the world market and transnational industry, rested on a supposed dissolution of nations. In his conclusion to *L'illusion économique*, anthropologist and demographer Todd is particularly severe on this vein of nonsense. Not only are nation-states refusing to dissolve, he points out, they are both reviving and proliferating. And for good reason. Although regimented and repressed by the Cold War era, nationalism is constitutive of man's *social* nature. The era was an aberration, nationality is not. Also, a return of agency and political confidence depends upon such revival: 'The real problem and solution take us back to the anthropological and cultural foundations of the (economic) system', he writes. In response to 'market forces', protection is as inevitable now as it ever was, and demands a revalidation of societal cohesion and trust – that is, of national identity and interests.

Nor is this recognition confined to anthropology or high theory. Saner economists have been wrestling with the contradiction for years, and reaching the same conclusion by a different route. Perhaps the most

---

61 The most penetrating deconstruction of global economania is Justin Rosenberg's *The Follies of Globalisation Theory* (Verso 2000). Pursuing his earlier analyses of international relations in *The Empire of Civil Society* (Verso 1994), he is especially hard on New Labour's leading prophet, Anthony Giddens. A space-time metaphysic has come to be deployed by such social scientists, to give the impression of a practically cosmic process over-riding statehood and sovereignty alike. It causes nations to dissolve alongside the 'Westphalian system', a mythical structure of pre-Third-Way darkness awaiting the transforming touch of Blair.

influential work in this direction has been that of Dani Rodrik at Harvard University. His *Has Globalisation Gone Too Far?* (1997) is a well-documented questioning of globalisation nostrums, arguing that 'the most serious challenge for the world economy in the years ahead lies in making globalisation compatible with domestic social and political stability – or to put it even more directly, in ensuring that international economic integration does not contribute to domestic *dis*integration'. His later essay *The New Global Economy and Developing Countries: Making Openness Work* (1999) is another penetrating overview of the same theme, which ends by placing great emphasis upon politics: 'It may be true . . . that the information revolution and the globalisation of production necessitates novel forms of governance. We need to figure out what these forms of governance are and how we can institute them' (p.152). However, given that for the time being 'national governments are all we have', it would be folly to give them up, or to assume in some ideological sense that all are doomed or in retreat.

On the contrary, many are awakening and advancing. They are finding their feet under the conditions of a more globalised world and a more open economic order. If we return again to the UK and France, the difficulty of Rodrik's 'domestic disintegration' is at once clear. He warns against thinking all integration is unconditionally good, but still assumes all disintegration must be bad. Fortunately this is not the case. Some states merit domestic disintegration, while for others it may indeed be tragic (the one to which he pays most attention is Mexico). There is no automatic common measure. The British multinational society discussed above is a painful specimen of life-support survivalism, while its constituent parts – Northern Ireland, Scotland, Wales, the London region – are examples of countries that would probably succeed far better in the new global context. The Irish Republic is of course already *the* outstanding success story of this kind. Here, 'disintegration' means liberation, and the building (or for the Scots, rebuilding) of new nations, more demo-cratic as well as more national. What Britain is breaking up into is not, or is not necessarily, a cluster of exclusionary nationalities – its 'novel forms of governance' are far more likely to be outward-looking versions of civic nationalism.

In the 1960s, opposition was both inspired and crippled by 'inter-nationalism'. This was a Utopian exhalation of protest, primarily from the Left, which set a purer single world against the dire hostilities of colonial-ism and imperial statehood. Renouncing 'the nation' then meant a somersault into the stratosphere of purged humanity (as endorsed by Moscow, Trotsky, Kropotkin or Jesus). Forty years on, internationalism has, as 'globalisation', turned into the profane burden of daily existence. Then, nobody could reach it save in dreams. Now, no one can escape it for a second. Morning prayers to The Invisible Hand, midday prostration before the IMF and the WTO, then the eventide confessional of competi-tive shortcomings: such is the Captivity of the new millennium. And as Todd maintains, advance to renewed national communities represents the sole way out.

Over this watershed, the profile of 'nationalism' is as different as that of the former *Internationale*. In the one world of post-1989, humanity has had no option but to re-encounter nature. The resultant *rapprochement* is with pre-history, and the bases of human society: '*Nous sommes ici au coeur du mystère humain*', as Todd puts it. But the 'mystery' to which he points is the transcendence of blood relations, not retreat back into them: the construction of civic nationalism, rather than the reiteration of eth-nicity, or of mythologies of ancestry and belonging. After the prolonged dearth of the later twentieth century, the pressures of a common fate are forcing such political transcendence. But 'transcend' means, precisely, recognition and acceptance for the purposes of reconstruction – not dis-avowal and suppression in the name of a detached reason. Metaphysical economism was reason at its most detached – the dregs of a misinter-preted Enlightenment, rather than its expansion.[62]

This alteration has of course been drawn to the notice of the world public by the 'anti-globalisation movement' of the last few years, from the 1998 Seattle demonstrations down to the huge meeting at Porto Alegre, Brasil, in February 2002. But one need no longer refer to it alone, or to the various 'new politics' movements and research initiatives which have sprung up since the 1990s, in order to appreciate what is under way. I sus-pect we are only now experiencing something of that liberation, that sense of exploding possibility and achievement which was lacking in the 1980s – or which was not then allowed expression by the gelid assumptions of a world still thawing out from the Cold War.

That this movement has been in some respects incoherent, utopian, anarchic (and so on) is surely not surprising. After all, it opposes a dogma marked by over-coherence, cringing uniformity and contempt for the imag-ination, and for all forms of unmarketable spontaneity. Like Stalinism before it, neo-liberal economism rested upon exorcism of the political will. It con-ceived politics instrumentally: what farthers the gospel is healthy, what does not is mad, or 'backward', or irrational, or simply evil. The economical meta-physics of Leninism and Friedmanite capitalism alike rejected the autonomy of politics and culture as a threat their integrity – that is, to the integrity of what were actually historical systems of exploitation and control, imagining themselves as eternal (God, Nature or capital-H History).

---

62 The bedraggled 'Enlightenment' endlessly brandished by defenders of economical New Faith was in truth a cramped and transitional structure, analogous to the 'Industrial Revolution' of British legend. Recent re-examinations of its origins like Jonathan Israel's *Radical Enlightenment: Philosophy and the Making of Modernity, 1650-1750* (Oxford University Press 2001) show how disparate and qualified the Reason of that period actually was.

The 2002 Davos Conference was staged in New York as a tribute to the city, with a good deal of added ceremony (including a visit from Mr and Mrs Bill Gates). On 9 February 2002 the *New York Times* published an amusing account of one of the sessions. The chieftains of global capitalism were now perturbed enough by protests and adverse publicity to invite *a critic* to address them. Professor Rodrik was summoned from Harvard University and awarded three minutes to explain himself. Ten minutes would obviously have been excessive. Five? The assumption must have been that whatever such a fellow might utter in 300 clock seconds could also be said in 180; so that was that.

The Professor seems to have acquitted himself very well in the circumstances. *Times* reporter Louis Uchitelle reported his opening salvo: 'There is no single, simple model of globalisation'. This was the equivalent of casually dropping a copy of *The Satanic Verses* in the Shrine of Mecca: deadly stuff, in the context of a self-admiration society. Dogmatic economism has always relied entirely on single-mindedness and simplification. Such monomania then enables devotees to claim 'radicalism' as their distinguishing badge, and hence dismiss all opponents as fudgers, fossils, romantics and has-beens.

Uchitelle's account quotes Rodrik (talking very fast, one must assume) as going on to give an example. Millions of people over the globe have been showing signs of taking 'globalisation' uncomfortably literally, by deciding to move themselves and their families across frontiers, over mountain passes, in leaky boats on shark-infested seas, through road and rail tunnels, hidden in aircraft holds and container trucks, almost always without the required nation-state paperwork. Such unruly conduct is ignored by the prayer-books of the World Trade Organisation. It failed even to mention 'labour mobility' at its conclave in Qatar last November. Rodrik pointed out the absurdity. Everybody knows mass migration will continue, and almost certainly escalate when the present economic recession ends. The world's remaining countryside is determined to get to town. So, why not seek a new international agreement which would 'allow people from poorer countries to work for three to five years in rich countries . . . sending home part of their pay and eventually going home themselves to use their newly acquired skills to help spur economic development there'?

I mention this as one example among many of the kind of modest proposal which might assist recovery from the prelude to globalisation the world has been forced through since 1989. Just as the steps needed to reform the UK are straightforward rather than New, so those on the level of international relations are pragmatic, rather than 'radical' in the oniric sense of Napoleonic neo-liberalism. The point of both must be to prosecute the democratic revolution which has now gathered strength in the background since the 1960s, replacing dictatorships with a majority of (at least) representative régimes and pretend-democracies. Anti-globalisation is inherently democratic, and (I would argue) inherently nationalist in orientation – but in the sense of civic-popular, rather than ethnic and exclusionary. Democracy is a matter of constitutions; and as Jean-Jacques Rousseau recognised, constitutions have to be particular as well as reflecting general values and ideas. They require communities, or 'nations' (and sometimes – more often than not) they also help to construct or reform these, in order to attain valid political existence. Contrary to the twentieth century's fixed belief, the civic rather than the ethnic is the foundation of societal nature.

I suggested earlier that the 'break-up' of the archipelago could have been a future-oriented exercise – a 'test-bed' of emancipation from fossil-sovereignty, providential obsessions and the abscesses of racialism. As such, Britain might have been a more modest and marginal model of change – somewhere in the same spectrum as the Baltic states, the Low Countries, New Zealand, South Africa and parts of Latin America.

Prominent in Göran Therborn's 'decent periphery', as it were, rather than a pivot and First Lieutenant of Freedom. However, Blair's New Labour only flirted coyly with such notions, then scuttled back into the bunker of Greatness whenever the dust on the ornaments was disturbed. Only with the coming collapse of the bunker itself is some successor likely to take reform more seriously.

APPENDIX

An exchange of letters between Tom Nairn and Yasmin Alibhai-Brown, the British-Asian journalist and broadcaster, *Independent* columnist and author of *Who Do We Think We Are?* (Penguin 2000). The debate was commissioned by a Scottish newspaper, the *Sunday Herald*, in March 2000, but never published.

Dear Tom,

How British Are We? is the question we are asked to address in this exchange. And yet you have already declared Britain terminally ill, in need perhaps of mercy killing to end its suffering. Your book *After Britain* is so exuberant in its certainties, so wonderfully seductive and intensely intellectual, so, so erudite (I am ashamed to say that many of your allusions made me feel small, inferior and ill-read) that it is hard to resist its dazzling imperatives. This half-way house of controlled devolution cannot be sustained. A new free Scotland must be created to redress a great historical injustice. The process is unstoppable you say, and quote Ian Bell saying that the Scottish national memory had been reclaimed. As an ex-subject of the British Empire, which the Scots enthusiastically participated in of course, how can I fail to rejoice in this? It evokes in me many profound memories. That reclamation kindled similar passions in India and in East Africa where I was born. I went to Makerere University and joined other idealists who knew freedom was more than replacing one flag with another. We were determined to write our lost and suppressed history and by doing so liberate the locked and miserable souls of subject people. So a part of me, which has been lying down for too long, is stirred by your spirit and words. But the larger part of me is frightened by the implications: the ease with which you give up on the British nation (as it is today and not as it once was) and your sanguine belief that Scottish nationalism will not necessarily produce excluding, mean and dangerous impulses among those who most want to see a separate Scotland. The irony you see, Tom, is that black and Asian Britons today feel more deeply about their British identity than any of the indigenous groups. Once, not that long ago, this identity represented humiliation. We had blue British passports (kept in bank safe-deposit boxes with the most precious family jewels) which since 1968 had been rendered worthless, denying us the basic rights of citizenship in this country. We were never accepted as of this island. I am still asked every week where I come from and why I speak such good English. But in the last few years we have embraced and transformed Britishness and by doing so redefined the British identity. Now Scottish, Welsh and English nationalists want to take this away and relegate us to those lesser beings who have no ancestral connections to this land. Talk of the four nations is the beginning of this process. In my book *Who Do We Think We Are?*, I am fighting for this revivified and, yes, cosmopolitan state where people like me are at the heart of it and not in the margins. I do not want to see cultural, racial and now post-devolution fragmentation which is likely to destroy this new emerging British identity and replace it with something simpler and sweeter, where we can all pretend that the 'other' will never confront our own complacencies and there will be no need for honest contemplations. That, I fear, is where you might be taking us.

Yours,

Yasmin

Dear Yasmin,

Thank you very much for your comments, and your critique of the risks inherent in nationalist politics. You and other black and Asian Britons claim to have 'embraced and transformed Britishness' and so begun redefining the British identity. But now you seem to fear this very transformation may leave you helpless against the revived, post-British identities of the Scots, the Welsh, the Irish and (most important) the English. The heedless, exclusive nationalisms of the archipelago natives might then reproduce your East African dilemma – only this time few will have still another passport locked away with the family jewels. So, the previously colonised victims of British Imperialism have become quite keen to save what's left of Britain – provided it is changed or 'cosmopolitan' enough to suit them, like London and other parts of (mainly) Southern England.

Scotland, Wales and Northern Ireland are countries of massive (and still continuing) emigration. They all suffer from absurdly small immigrant numbers, and so have not benefited from the cross-fertilising, transformative influences you describe. In a time of reawakening this is a severe handicap. As you must have noticed, not a single representative of black or Asian Scots got into parliament at our first elections. Some blame attaches to Scottish Labour Party selection procedures. But of course most of it lies unavoidably in a one-per cent electorate, severely divided within itself. This is only the ancient unfairness Norman Davies has described in *The Isles*. The principal 'white tribe' not only has most of the population, the fertile land, the economy, the international status and armed force; today, it gets most of the immigrants too!

Self-government – I would prefer to say just 'independence' – is one way of trying to counterbalance the built-in 85 per cent English hegemony that 'Britain' once stood for. Haywire fringes apart, I don't really see much heedless or exclusivist passion at work there. It would be more accurate to say there's a mounting determination in the periphery to *renegotiate* Britain – to create a looser, more equal and less informal common roof. 'Nationalism' is a way of doing this. It means standing on one's own feet, not communing with a genetic spirit-world. And so far, it doesn't strike me as much different from what you mean by 'transforming Britishness'. Peripheral national movements and minority interests ought to be allies, not ideological foes. But there is a serious obstacle in the way. 'Renegotiation' implies consenting parties willing to negotiate, and one of these – the most important one – is still missing: England. I suspect what you really fear is a nativist English reaction to our assorted provocations, which might rebound upon you as well as on us.

Where I disagree absolutely with you is on your remedy. It advocates clinging to the old Devil for fear of something worse. The British realm needs replacing, not 'transforming'. Here your language unintentionally colludes with that of the *ancien régime*, always eager for gradual changes guaranteed to prop up conservative customs and power. Blairism is now into this 'blessèd plot' stuff up to its neck. The prospect of indefinite office has convinced him of Middle England's indifference to constitutional matters. The worrying thing about your position is not what *you* mean by it, but how this Anglo-idiot élite is bound to read it: for the latter, 'keeping Britain' now means Ken Livingstone falling under one of his own buses, a Clone-House of Lords and first-past-the-post until Kingdom come (in the person of Prince Willie). This is the real fall of Britishness, in more than rhetoric. But is it really inconceivable that a new, all-colours, thoroughly civic *English* nationalism could react against such traditions in decay? I don't know whether that means all-English or regional-plus-minority English. Your argument implies the latter, and I hope you're right.

I mean, *you've got to be right*. 'Four-nations' talk to me is no conventicle of ancestor-worshippers, from which newcomers will be excluded. It's a way of looking forward to a different Britain, whether as a confederation, an association, or simply as equal members of the European Union. A genuine community of citizens is the only real safeguard for incomers and minorities – and this is exactly what Old Britain in its pickle-preserved state is not. Is not and (I must say in spite of your case for the contrary) never will be. Striving to keep the latter going is the one thing certain to bring the wolves into the house. It wouldn't be the first time that the Left had dismissed nationality-politics, only to see it fall straight into the paws of a resurgent Right slavering about come-backs, former glories and family values.

I don't believe for a moment that new-English identity is fated to take that road. Were that so, I don't think that you newcomers could have succeeded in changing it, as you have. Yet anyone can see how uncertain you feel about the permanence and reliability of this achievement. That's why you feel we shouldn't rock the boat. But I think Charter 88 got it right: yes, it is time to rock the boat – the boat we are all in – with a more serious constitutional revolution, in which England (theirs *and* yours) participates alongside the rest of us.

All the best

Tom

Dear Tom,

It is extraordinary how differently we see Britishness today. You see it as an Old Devil. I see it as subversive of all nationalisms and fundamentalisms, undergoing changes it barely understands, as I have said in *Who Do We Think We Are?* The transformations I embrace with passion are not those of devolution, but you know that already, not least because of the reasons you mention in your letter. The brand-new, young, rediscovered Scottish nation, locked as it is in an ethnic redefinition of itself, found no space for the visible communities who have lived there for generations. Without even noticing (the greatest insult I suppose) they relegated black Britons to second-class status. Ditto Wales. These are the real, proven dangers of the Scotland you want. I embrace quite a different vision which cannot survive in these smaller, stronger nations, not even if a powerful and popular civic bond is promoted by political leaders. My vision includes the *Telegraph* having to accept that Indian food now defines this nation. It is *Goodness Gracious Me* and *East is East*, which are proudly New British. They could never be Scottish, Welsh or English. It means an Indian director, Shekhar Kapoor, making an exquisitely honest film about Elizabeth the First, the most English of monarchs, and then being feted as a British success. I see this Britishness as capable of moral challenges to groups which have become oppressive under the hiding places provided by traditional multiculturalism and of getting them to see themselves as part of this country rather than visitors who will one day go back home to countries long left behind which mean little to their children. Politically active black and Asian people like myself have spent years fighting against shrinking and simplistic identities which many in our communities are drawn to. You and yours are engaged in exactly the opposite project. And yes there are the restive English (remember Defoe who said 'From this amphibious ill born mob began, that vain, ill-natured thing, the Englishman') on whose lands most of us live. What has been unleashed cannot be contained again but it can be circumscribed and made less appealing by the invention of a better, broader identity, that of New Britishness.

Yours,

Yasmin

Dear Yasmin,

So you still feel the Old Devil has become a Nurse! As you put it to begin with – Britain 'as it once was, not as it is today'. But of course this where we go on disagreeing: I think it still is *essentially* 'as it once was'. Blairism is Hormone Replacement Therapy, not revolution. Neither we on the periphery nor you in the heartland can forge this New Britishness. Only the English majority can accomplish that, by combining more serious constitutional change with greater determination on the European side. They have to become Europeans for deep-political reasons – not via Gordon Brown's miserable list of economic pretexts, in three or thirteen years time (or never). With all its failings, European Union remains the best example of nationalities combining to escape their past – and enshrining their new formula in written-constitutional terms (which alone will provide the long-range guarantees I think you want). That's what they already think in the Republic of Ireland. I hope it's what we will come to believe in the Republic of Scotland.

I wish one could say 'and in the Republic of England' also – but so much of the majority *ethnos* seems not to want this direction at all. It prefers to tread water and place its hope in significant yet secondary 'transformations', like the films you mention, or the ascent of Asians in the British media (incidentally, just as striking in Scotland as down South). *East is East* is a brilliant *historical* film portraying the England of a few years back, and I agree things have altered for the better. Having lived in London at the height of Powellism, I need no persuading about that. And yet (as you plainly fear) things could still slide backwards. That's what I meant about the wolves. We do have a few mangy specimens scrabbling around the dustbins up here, but (inevitably) the main pack is near your back door, in England. Don't blame us for their howling! A renewed English identity is required to disable them, rather than Tony Blair's rehash of old Britland.

All the best,

Tom

INDEX

Alibhai-Brown, Yasmin 106, 163–70
Ancram, Michael, Earl of 40
Anderson, Perry 32n.19
apathy, voter 2, 3–4, 5, 57–9, 68, 82, 96
Ashdown, Paddy 93
asylum-seekers 8, 107

Barker, Tony
  Ruling by Task Force 42
Barnett, Anthony 1, 4
  Iron Britannia 51
Basildon, Essex 72
Bell, Steve and Homer, Brian
  Chairman Blair's Little Red Book 81
Bew, Paul 113, 114, 117
Blackburn, Robin 25
Blair, Tony 1, 2, 4, 5, 6, 9, 11, 13, 14–15, 25, 28–9, 30, 31, 37, 44, 48, 49, 56, 65, 69, 77, 81, 82, 83, 95, 96, 127, 133, 138–46, 148
  personal background 141–2

Blairism 4, 23–6, 30, 32, 39, 53, 54–5, 70, 74–7, 82, 84, 123, 125
British National Party 110, 123
British-Irish Council 85, 111, 112–13
Brown, Gordon 4, 43, 44, 78, 83, 90, 92–3, 95, 96, 100, 125, 133, 141, 144–5
Brown, Nicholas 64
Bulpitt, Jim 19–21, 52, 64, 70, 97
Burke, Edmund 41, 69, 70, 99, 112, 114–15, 117

capitalism 34–5, 153–5
Charter 88 77, 78
Chevènement, Jean-Pierre 131
Chirac, Jacques 133
Christian Democracy 27
Churchill, Winston 38, 39, 40, 51–3, 151
Clinton, Bill 139
Cohen, Nick 3
Colley, Linda 28, 29

Colombani, Jean-Marie
  Les infortunes de la République
    89, 124, 129, 130–32
Communism 21–2
  Fall of 147, 150–51, 154–5
Conservatism 13, 22, 24, 40–41, 47,
    110, 135
Conservatives 18–19, 30, 44, 47, 77,
    102, 107, 117
constitutionalism, British 24, 26,
    58, 77–8, 79, 117
Cook, Robin 118, 125
Crewe, Ivor 91n.42

Davies, Norman
  The Isles 88, 129, 135
Davos Conference 160
De Valera, Eamon 99–100
Dennis, Nigel
  Cards of Identity 123
depoliticisation 59, 61
Deutscher, Isaac 74
Devolution 38, 50, 73, 83–9, 92–5,
    100, 101, 102, 104, 131, 133,
    145
  see also individual countries
Dewar, Donald 84
Diana, Princess 79
Dörler, Bernd 7

Edwards, Ruth Dudley
  The Faithful Tribe 115
election 2001 1, 3–5, 12, 16, 29–30,
    43, 50, 57–8, 75, 85
  media coverage 5–6

Empson, William
  Argufying 122
  'Missing dates' 71
  Seven Types of Ambiguity 119
ethnicity 98–111
Euro-currency 43–4, 128–9, 133,
    143
Europe 43, 133–4, 135, 136,
    137
European Union 14–15, 43–4,
    128–9, 133

foot-and-mouth disease 1–2, 3–4,
    64–6, 75–6, 103
Foreign Policy 62
Fortini, Franco
  'The Eaves' 138
France 25, 51, 83, 89, 102, 124,
    125–6, 127, 129, 130–33, 152,
    157
Frank, Thomas 147

Garton Ash, Timothy
  'The Old United Kingdom is
    Dead' 10–11, 14, 104
Gaulle, Charles de 15, 83, 136
Germany 136, 137
Gladstone, William 117
globalisation 13, 34n.21, 62, 63, 76,
    80, 121, 129, 147, 150, 151,
    154, 155–7, 159–61
Gramsci, Antonio
  Prison Notebooks 21

Hague, William 40, 44, 102

Hailsham, Quintin Hogg, Lord
   The Dilemma of Democracy 14
   'The Nation and the
      Constitution' 17, 24, 25, 26,
      75, 78
Hall, Stuart
   'The Moving Right Show' 21–2,
      75, 105, 144
Harris, Robert 75, 76
Hassan, Gerry and McCormick, Jim
   'Blair: the Future of Britain and
      the Britishness' 92
'Heath' 6
Hitler, Adolf 100
Hobsbawm, Eric 45
House of Lords 86

identity
   national 12–17, 24–6, 28, 29, 31,
      33, 35–8, 40, 45–6, 56–7, 60,
      67, 71–2, 73–4, 75, 77, 98,
      99, 101, 105, 116–23, 126,
      139, 141
   dual 104
   see also ethnicity
Ignatieff, Michael 128
industrialism 34–5
Industry Standard Europe 61
Ingham, Geoffrey
   Capitalism Divided 34–5, 52, 53
internationalism 158
Ireland, Republic of 36, 44, 62, 157

Jenkins, Lord 55–6, 122
Jenkins, Simon 54

Johnson, R.W. 82, 85–6, 87, 92,
   117
Jones, Nicholas
   The Control Freaks 42

Kavanagh, Dennis 18, 30–31,
   64
Kennedy, Charles 94
Keynes, J.M. 153
Kinnock, Neil 100, 141
Klein, Joe 29, 138–9, 141, 142
   'Letter from London' 67–8

Labour Party 17, 39, 77, 142–3
Le Monde diplomatique 124–5
Liberal Democrats 93, 94
Little England 37, 104–5
Lloyd-George, David 57, 99
Lukacs, John
   Five Days in London, May 1940
      51, 52

Macmillan, Harold 31–2
Macwhirter, Iain
   'Will the Real Tony Blair Stand
      Up?' 143
Major, John 23, 70, 77
Mandelson, Peter 4, 54, 70, 75
Mann, Thomas
   Mario and the Magician 6
Marr, Andrew
   The Day Britain Died 11
Marwick, Arthur
   *Britain in Our Century: Images
      and Controversies* 29, 31

Marx, Karl 34, 99, 151, 153, 155
  'The Elections in England –
    Tories and Whigs' 88
Marxism 34, 35, 151
McElvoy, Anne 54, 82, 102–3, 104
McKibbin, Ross 60–61, 63, 64, 74
McKie, David 57
McNeill, William
  The Fall of Great Powers' 109–10
media 65, 74–6
  election coverage 5–6
Middle England 85, 90, 94
Miliband, David 67–8
Millennium Dome 53–4, 144
Milosevic, Slobodan 100
Milward, Alan
  The European Rescue of the
    Nation-state 133
Mitterrand, François 102, 126, 131
Monarchy 79, 81
Morrison, John 73, 145–6
  Reforming Britain 77, 78, 80
Mount, Ferdinand 58–9
  The National Interest 111

Nairn, Tom
  'Farewell Britannia' 111, 113, 114
  After Britain 126
Napoleon, Louis 25
nationalism 8, 13, 50, 104, 107, 135,
    136, 156, 158
New Labour 1, 2, 3, 5, 25, 50, 54–5,
    57, 66, 68, 73, 78–80, 84–5, 88,
    90–92, 94, 95, 96, 135, 148,
    155, 162

Northern Ireland 43, 87, 89,
    111–18, 133, 144, 157
Norton, Philip
  Strengthening Parliament 80

O'Brien, Conor Cruise
  Memoir 113
Orwell, George
  The Lion and the Unicorn 120
  1984 74

Paine, Thomas 115, 116
Parekh, Bikhu, Lord
  The Future of Multi-Ethnic
    Britain: the Parekh Report
    98, 101, 105, 108, 109
Patten, Christopher 19, 50
Pempel, T.J.
  Uncommon Democracies: The
    One Party Dominant
    Régimes 26–8, 30, 42
populism 20, 22, 24, 59, 63
Portillo, Michael 47
Powell, Enoch 119
Prescott, John 95
Purdie, Bob 115

race relations 8, 37, 98, 107–8
radicalism 48, 55, 86
Ramonet, Mr 124–5
Rawnsley, Andrew
  'What a bunch of miserable
    winners!' 96–7
recession 2
referenda 94, 143

reform
    constitutional 50, 77, 79–81,
        83–9, 94, 104, 108, 122, 136
    electoral 55–6
    political 73, 83
Reid, John 4, 9, 84
Rentoul, John 141–2
Reynaud, Paul 51
Richards, Steve
    'They look so fed up, you
        wouldn't think they'd just
        won an election' 95, 96
Riddell, Peter
    'Be Worried, Mr Blair, be Very,
        Very Worried' 95, 96
Ridley, Nicholas 40
Rodrik, Dani 160–61
    Has Globalisation Gone Too Far?
        157
    *The New Global Economy and
        Developing Countries:
        Making Openness Work*
        157
Rosenberg, Justin
    *The Follies of Globalisation
        Theory* 156n.61
Rousseau, Jean-Jacques 161
Rubinstein, W.D. 36

'Save the Union' movement 89
Scandinavia 61, 128, 137
Scotland 43, 84, 87, 93, 103, 111,
        113–14, 133, 144, 157, 158
Scottish National Party 89
Scruton, Roger 118

Siedentop, Larry 136
Smith, Adam 153
Smith, John 78, 100
Socialism 21–2
    British 50, 55, 56, 122
Stalin, Joseph 99
Stern
    'The English Patient' 7
Stevenson, John 99

Taylor, A.J.P. 97
Thatcher, Margaret 17, 18–19, 23,
        26, 27, 40, 41, 51, 64, 69, 78,
        83, 95, 141, 153
Thatcherism 18, 19, 22, 26–7, 73,
        74–5, 155
Therborn, Göran 34n.21
    'Europe in the Twenty-first
        Century 137, 162
Third Way 5, 23, 25, 60, 77, 125,
        148, 155
Tidrick, Kathryn 50
    Empire and the English Character
        30, 52, 56, 63, 68
Tocqueville, Alexis de 61, 63, 125,
        131
Todd, Emmanuel 131n.52
    L'illusion économique ('The
        Economic Illusion') 147,
        148, 149, 153, 156, 158
'Touchstone Issues' 145
Toynbee, Polly and Walker, David
    Did Things Get Better? 94
tradition 35–6, 43
Trimble, David 116

Uchitelle, Louis 160
USA 2, 15, 28, 38, 76, 152, 153
   Constitution 28, 152

Védrine, Hubert 76
   Les cartes de la France à l'heure de
      la mondialisation 127–8, 129
Von Hayek, Friedrich 155

Walden, George 146
Wales 43, 87, 103, 111, 133, 144, 157

Wasson, Ellis 140
Watkins, Alan 8–9
Whitelaw, William 40
Wilson, Sir Harold 17
Wingfield-Stratford, Esmé
   Foundations of British Patriotism
      60, 62
World War II 51–2, 151

Young, Hugo 106